W9-AMA-427

The Accidental Teacher

Life Lessons from my Silent Son

An Autism Memoir

Annie Lubliner Lehmann

authorHOUSE®

AuthorHouse™
1663 Liberty Drive, Suite 200
Bloomington, IN 47403
www.authorhouse.com
Phone: 1-800-839-8640

First published by AuthorHouse 4/24/2008

ISBN: 978-1-4343-7696-1 (sc)

Printed in the United States of America
Bloomington, Indiana

This book is printed on acid-free paper.

"We understand backward but live forward"

Soren Kierkegaard

Table of Contents

This book is lovingly dedicated to my son
Jonah
And all those with autism who
speak volumes without saying a word

Acknowledgments

From the time I drafted the first words of this book until I sent the completed manuscript to the printer, I was ambivalent about its publication. After all, the relationship between a parent and child is sacred and I wondered if I was violating my son's privacy by putting to page what happened behind closed doors. But I believe that what I have learned on this journey, which continues, is valuable and worth sharing. Most compelling among the lessons is that adversity breeds wisdom.

You hear this from the cancer survivor who, after treatment, talks about appreciating things like never before; the ex-con who gains insight and given a second chance, rises to the top; the abused person who confronts her demons and is primed to rescue others from the place she once stood.

While autism may figure prominently in this book, the work is more about self-discovery than illness and offers insights that result from raising any child, especially one with autism.

Writing this book has been a labor of love, and from the start my intention was to use it to share, educate and raise funds for autism research. Some of the names have been changed to protect the privacy of individuals. With the help and support of many people, I never lost sight of these goals. There are many to thank.

As Holocaust survivors my parents, Helen and Jack Lubliner (of blessed memory), exemplified strength of character and taught me the meaning of survival. Their innate wisdom, kindness and ability to rise above life's cruelties have been an ongoing source of inspiration.

Without my son Jonah there would be no book. The eldest of my three children, he not only introduced me to parenthood, but also to a corner of life that, given the choice, I would never have known. He has given me many gifts, among them, a lens through which to see the world.

David and Ruth, Jonah's younger siblings, allowed me the privilege of parenting normal children. I thank them for adding so much to my life, giving me a reason to buy my first minivan and for having the sense to say things like "every family needs a bachelor uncle."

My husband Michael has added a new dimension to the words friend, husband and partner. I thank G-d for gracing me with a husband who has helped me build our one-of-a-kind family and realize so many of my lifelong dreams. I consider myself fortunate to share this often-wild ride with someone so patient, kind and caring.

To Marvin Margolis, M.D., Ph.D., a teacher, friend and inspiration who encouraged the writing of this book. Thanks for the insight and for allowing me to see that sadness can be a sizable piece of life's pie without eclipsing joy and meaning.

Finally, the list would not be complete without mentioning the following friends and family, each who has contributed to this project either by offering encouraging words, a shoulder to lean on or took me for a walk or coffee when I was bleary eyed from too much time in front of the computer.

A much deserved thanks goes to my cheerleader sister Sandra Weitz who taught me never to take "no" for an answer; close friends and readers Phyllis Barax, Shirley Rubin, Helene Weiss, Renee Wohl, Netanya Weiss Hoffman, Alison Hochbaum, and my agent, Nancy Crossman, who supported this project from the start.

Introduction

Historically, 1983 was a minor blip on the calendar of the century, not one of those standout years that adds inches to already overly thick history books. Yet at our house, the most life-altering event would occur with the birth of our first child.

My husband Michael and I had been married for two years, enjoyed the pleasures of childless couplehood and were eager to add a new dimension to our lives. Fortunately, nature cooperated and we were able to choose the time we thought best to start a family. When a plus sign appeared in the window of the early pregnancy test, we were off and running, naively treating expectant parenthood as something at which to excel.

As my waistline expanded so did our library, which became home to volumes about pregnancy, nutrition and child development. We attended prenatal classes, religiously followed the rules of how to have a healthy baby and became acquainted with the best of in baby paraphernalia. I enjoyed my pregnancy—intrigued by all the physical changes, the green light to self-indulge and the newfound attention my big belly seemed to precipitate.

When common worries about the baby's well being surfaced, my husband, a physician, reassured me with statistics. Without a history of medical problems or abnormalities in either of our families, it was reasonable to expect that our child would be a healthy Joe or Joan. As it turned out he would be neither. Our son Jonah would be born with autism, a disability that would transform our lives in ways we never could have anticipated.

Adding any child to the family mix has an enormous impact—just listen to old marrieds talk about the BC (before children) and AC (after children) phases of their lives. Yet as life changing and challenging as it is to rear a child in today's super-paced world, the mantle of parenthood bears enormous additional weight when the child has special needs. Autism is an especially greedy disability, interfering with communication and social interaction.

According to a January, 2008 article published in *The New York Times*, "up to one in 150 children born in the United States show some evidence of the social and learning difficulties that characterize autism, and scientists understand very little about how or why those problems develop." A February, 2005 article in *The Wall Street Journal* reported that the Centers for Disease Control and

Prevention concluded that autism "increased tenfold over the past decade."

How have these skyrocketing statistics been explained? Some experts point to broadening criteria, increased awareness and toxic exposures. But as far back as 2002, a front-page article in *The New York Times* was headlined, "Increase in autism baffles scientists . . . . California Study says increase is real but cause unknown." Jonah, it turned out, was at the starting gate of a growing epidemic.

Though we recognized that something was wrong early on, it took almost four years for us to learn the official name for what we were seeing. Jonah was atypical, a conundrum. His developmental delays were obvious, but he didn't display the rigidity or resistive tantrumming often associated with autism. In fact, he was overly docile and seemingly indifferent to his surroundings. What we didn't realize was that he had already begun setting up shop in his own faraway world.

Once we had a label for his peculiar behaviors and delays, we began researching the subject. Internet use was in its infancy and information was relatively limited. Books on the subject were primarily daily journals or dry academic texts with lots of language about "refrigerator mothers." I searched for information everywhere, but what I looked for, I couldn't find.

I wanted books about the day-to-day navigating—the truth about what our vulnerable population of parents was being sold. I wanted someone who had weathered the storm to warn me of the pitfalls without platitudes or sugarcoating; I wanted and needed kitchen table wisdom. That is why I have written this book.

More than two decades of having Jonah in my life has put me at a new vantage point. I can look back and recount the emotional journey, which often felt like a dizzying rollercoaster ride; share where I've been, what I've seen and how my life has changed as a result. Facing adversity, I have learned, no matter what form it takes, breeds its own brand of wisdom.

Parts of this book, the challenges, bureaucracies, humor and bittersweet moments, will be familiar to those who know autism intimately. Yet I have learned that despite meeting similar designated criteria, each story, like each person with autism, is unique.

I am no autism expert, just a mother and soldier, one of many in an army of parents. There are many insights to share. My report comes from the front lines. Here is our story.

Missed
Milestones

What had been a charmed pregnancy would hit the first major bump in the road with the beginning of labor. Despite all my reading and supposed preparedness for childbirth, I would discover that, as with most things, first hand experience is the best teacher.

Though medically I had what was considered a run-of-the-mill labor, the drama of the delivery seemed much bigger than I'd expected. This was, after all, the lifetime event I was told would dwarf all others and cause me to become a rank and file "mother." I felt like I was the first woman on the planet to give birth, awestruck by the magnitude of the milestone.

At that time, use of anesthesia during delivery was discouraged. None in our class of first time mothers-to-be knew what to expect and agreed that an alert baby that was able to bond properly was far more important than relief from temporary pain. Generations of mothers had managed without drugs; why couldn't we? The birthing instructor's message was not subtle—good mothering was measured from the moment you went into labor and were asked to put the needs of the baby before your own. Even 36 hours of labor could not change my mind. This was no small feat considering that the first word I associate with "dentist" is "Novocain."

The homey surroundings of the birthing room became ridiculously irrelevant as I went into the final stage of delivery. I heard murmurs of "fetal distress" and was urged by my doctor to stop pushing. Yet the desire to bear down overwhelmed me. It was as if my body had disconnected from my will.

After what seemed like an endless series of blue-faced pushes, Jonah was born. His first Apgar score, which measures the physical health of a newborn, was disturbingly low. A quick slap however roused him so that he screamed, a piercing wail, which caused me to cry along with relief. Despite the ominous first signs, his second Apgar score rose to the low/normal range. I looked at the doctor and was relieved when I saw him smiling. I was giddy with the miracle of having become a mother to a seemingly perfect boy with the number of fingers and toes I'd prayed for. Swaddled in flannel and weighing a little more than a large roast beef, I cradled our newest family member, certain that I understood what mother-child bonding was about. But just as a wedding is not a marriage, giving birth doesn't confer a bond in the true sense of the word. That, I would eventually learn, takes years to understand.

Bearing the first male grandchild in our family was cause to celebrate. The balloon-bouquets and well-wishers kept coming, and everyone it seemed wanted to welcome home this little person who nursed heartily and fulfilled my girlhood fantasies. More than anything, I'd work hard to raise this little person to become a kind and caring human being, like this father.

Within a few days, however, we hit a detour. Jonah's skin turned golden, as though he'd been in the sun too long. If the jaundice he had was as common as everyone was saying, I didn't understand why I had not read more about it in my pregnancy books? Caused by an elevated bile pigment or bilirubin, the symptoms, I was repeatedly reassured, would remit spontaneously with time. But we had a deadline. As observant Jews, we circumcise and name our boys on the eighth day of life. In order to do this, however, the baby's bilirubin, our rabbi said, would have to drop below ten. Sun exposure and removing Jonah from breast milk might help but ultimately, we were told, nature needed to cooperate.

I fed Jonah formula and expressed milk regularly in order to maintain my nursing momentum. I could have simplified life by switching to the bottle entirely, but with my "natural is best" proclivities, giving up what was best for my baby was never a consideration. Instead of focusing on the health issue at hand, I foolishly concentrated on milk production and exhausted myself in the process. On some level I believed my effort was another way of proving my motherly devotion.

Jonah's bilirubin count stuttered downward but not enough for us to go ahead with a timely circumcision and baby naming. Though I didn't realize it at the time, this would become the first of many missed milestones.

In the public domain he was referred to as "boy Lehmann" until a month later when he was circumcised and given his rightful Jewish name, Moshe Jonah—or Jonah Moshe in English.

Both my parents survived the Holocaust but lost many family members whose names I wanted to use. Moshe was my mother's oldest brother, her protector and surrogate father throughout the war and someone she revered. We wanted to honor his memory but also wanted our child's name to mark a new beginning, unrelated to Jewish history's nightmarish chapter.

So we chose Jonah, which in Hebrew means "dove." Besides being a symbol of peace, this bird, without intending to, let Noah know that the world was ready to be repopulated after the Great Flood. We were also touched by the story of Jonah and the whale, with its message about growing through adversity. Jonah's crib became a small menagerie of stuffed doves and whales and each night I sang, "Jonah Moshe, his name it means a dove; he is the boy I love."

The idyllic days of new motherhood ended as suddenly as they had begun and I was on my own. The phone that rang unceasingly for weeks was silent and the endless stream of packages stopped arriving. I'd become just another mother with a baby. It didn't help that Jonah was born near the end of September, at the beginning of an early and bitter cold winter. We were living in Wisconsin, far from our families in New York, and I was lonely. Jonah's European—born pediatrician saw public places as germ-ridden and hazardous for young infants. I lacked the confidence to question the doctor's instructions. I had always thought of myself as an independent thinker but I had never been a mother. My stop-at-nothing friends with busy older children and tow-along infants thought I was crazy but when it came to my baby, I followed orders. My tendency to take advice to the extreme only made the situation worse. Consequently, I spent long gray days in an overheated apartment alone, folding laundry and watching clouds of water vapor rise over Lake Michigan.

Not surprisingly, I soon felt out of sorts. I couldn't sleep, afraid that I wouldn't hear Jonah's middle of the night crying. I had difficulty eating and spent each day teary-eyed and nervous. I wanted to be one of the smiling new mothers in magazine ads, well-rested, dressed in white, with a neatly tied satin ribbon in my silky salon-styled hair. Instead, I looked like a model for Planned Parenthood.

I was perennially red-eyed from too little sleep. My chest was swollen beyond recognition and none of my clothes fit. The few things I had to wear weren't very flattering and my hair, which often went unwashed, was pulled back in a tight ponytail. In simple terms I was a mess and at that point it had nothing to do with autism. It had everything to do with new motherhood and its continual demands. I felt like a constant siren was ringing inside my head and that I would never find equilibrium for myself, my baby or my poor husband who mistakenly married lunatic me.

Matters didn't improve much when I took Jonah for his four-week check up. Although his growth was impressive, 90th percentile in height and weight, the doctor expressed concern about his poor muscle tone.

"See," he said flopping his limp noodle legs. "It's too early to tell but he may have some problems. Go home and love him," he said casually ignoring the weight of what he had just suggested. I wanted to tell him how irresponsible he was for being so ambiguous, raising frightening questions without providing solid answers. Didn't he understand that what he said left me with nothing but a sense of dread? Perhaps I should have pushed harder, insisted that he share what he was thinking. My guess is that my backing off was a way of avoiding having to hear all the frightening possibilities.

After that visit, I kept a close eye on Jonah, hoping that the doctor had made a mistake. But unlike most mothers, who look for signs of intelligence, I watched for deficits and what they might mean.

Despite these distractions, Jonah was an easy baby to care for. He ate and slept well and had a sweet disposition. I remember my relief at seeing his excitement when I walked in the room. At least he didn't have autism, I told myself without knowing how broad the spectrum was. The irony was glaring.

By the time Jonah was three months old, I'd pulled myself together enough to take him for studio photographs. He had trouble grasping objects and lifting his head so I positioned him on his belly and tucked a small stuffed bear in his hand to help support his chin. He was strikingly beautiful dressed in a deep green velvet outfit, a gift that I had been saving for a special occasion. Interestingly, things like clothing were becoming increasingly irrelevant. Instead I focused on his sweet expression and tiny pillow cheeks that begged to be kissed. When the camera's light flashed, I experienced an unexplainable rush, a snapshot moment of my own. Jonah had been in my life for such a short time and yet I knew how thoroughly I loved him. I found it hard to believe that the flawlessly beautiful child I was looking at was mine.

As months passed, more and more milestones were being missed. Jonah couldn't roll over, hold his head up steadily or sit without support. He developed odd interests like swinging doors back and forth endlessly while lying on the floor. I learned that repetitive behaviors were called "perseverations." That would become the first of many words I would learn as part of an evolving "special needs" vocabulary.

Once again, when he turned six months, I took Jonah to be photographed. Still unable to sit up, I crouched behind him and grabbed his blue knit overalls tightly, supporting him from under the furry blanket on which he sat. The photographer's stock antics, funny noises and saying "boo," did not elicit a smile. Only a spinning toy I had brought along got his attention. The photographer was irritated by how long the session took and told me how difficult Jonah had been compared to others his age. I drove home devastated.

With each passing month Jonah's coordination and gross motor skills fell further behind. Family members and close friends rationalized by saying that he was bigger than most babies. According to them Jonah had "too much muscle mass" to move around. "Einstein was late to develop," they would say, hoping to allay my fears. And though everyone meant well, I knew that behind my back there were worried whispers.

Spending so much time alone with Jonah didn't help. A friend encouraged me to join a playgroup for mothers and young babies, which I did, reluctantly. I wasn't feeling particularly social and knew that the group was an excuse for housebound moms to get together. But I needed to get out of the house and distract myself from my worries. The women were nice and while the conversations may have been about sleep problems and great places to shop for kids' clothing, there was also an undercurrent of competitiveness. I heard a lot of "he's starting to creep," "she's interested in a cup." I had nothing to contribute. Instead of enjoying the social opportunity, I did what parents should never do, compared Jonah to others. I observed the other babies in the group and took mental notes, trying to get a handle on their developmental whereabouts. Week by week the gap between Jonah and his peers grew increasingly obvious.

Few things interested Jonah. He didn't protest when others grabbed his toys and seemed indifferent about everything but food. A good diagnostician might have recognized this over-passivity as a feature of his problem. Most of the other children in the group played by themselves or with others, checking periodically for their mothers' whereabouts. Jonah never seemed to care.

I identified with Jonah, and although it didn't matter to him, I felt like we were outsiders. I didn't want to indulge a "you-and-me-against-the-world mentality," and yet, that was how things seemed to be evolving. I'd take him home and fuss over his tiniest achievements. Watching him struggle made me appreciate the many complex steps sometimes necessary to complete the simplest tasks. Using a pincer grasp to pick up a single Cheerio, for example, was a very big deal at our house. I became Jonah's private cheerleader.

When the playgroup met for the last time we lined the babies up for a picture. Without being too obvious, I positioned Jonah at the far end of the couch for the extra support the armrest could provide. Already I was looking for ways to compensate for his deficits. A couple of weeks later I received a copy of the picture in the mail. I wasn't surprised to see nine toddlers seated in a variety of positions flanked by Jonah who had sagged forward and to the side.

In spite of my worries, I tried keeping life as normal as possible. We enjoyed family outings to the park and beach, and shared sweet unforgettable moments that young families so often do. I loved reading aloud to Jonah, carefully lingering on images and words and taking him to the pool, where he loved being swirled around in "motorboat go so fast" fashion.

What I enjoyed most, however, were the quiet, unremarkable moments of motherhood. Few things equaled the pleasure of rocking Jonah before bed, inspecting his physical perfection and watching his chest rise and fall while he drifted off. After putting him in his crib, I'd savor the lingering scent of his shampoo on my shoulder. Who would have guessed that I would be so grateful to Johnson&Johnson, the baby product manufacturer, for creating what I called the "great equalizer." Besides looking normal, Jonah got to smell like all the other babies I knew.

Still, it was a confusing and difficult time. Emotionally I was on edge. Every comment about Jonah seemed cruel and judgmental. I wanted desperately to be like other mothers who pushed strollers and swings in neighborhood parks without the self-consciousness. Talking openly about my concerns made me fearful, and Michael, not a worrier by nature, chose not to focus on what might be. He was happy with the way things were, even though it took him much longer to acknowledge obvious lapses and problems.

Family members vacillated – they either reassured us or expressed concern about Jonah's developmental delays. I could offer no answers to their worrisome questions. I, like everyone else, would have to wait and see.

When Jonah was 16 months old, we visited my parents in Florida. Jonah wasn't walking independently and their anxiety was obvious. Jonah and I were playing in the pool when my father's friend asked him Jonah's age. "Not even a year," my father responded.

I was hurt, but more enraged by the lie. I didn't want anyone trying to cover up for Jonah. "He is what he is," I later told my father, wanting and needing him to accept that his grandson might always be different than other children his age. I would make no excuses or deny what was true. If I had to accept the painful truth about my little boy I would get others to do the same. What better place to start than with my dad, Jonah's grandfather.

The "Alphabet Soup" of Special Needs

While many friends juggled motherhood with an ascent up the career ladder, I chose to be a stay-at-home mom. I always pictured myself as someone who would be happiest with a brood, playing in a toy-strewn room; crafting necklaces from fresh-picked daisies; baking brownies in a chocolate-splattered kitchen. I believed that I would be the sort of mother who would contentedly watch sun-illuminated dust particles settle on the furniture, using my observations to explain the sun's place in our solar system. Essentially, I wanted to create for my children, what I, as a child, would have liked to have had.

What I imagined however, had nothing to do with what actually occurred. The role I thought I would play was not designed for the Type A personality I was, and accepting this rather than judging myself a failure would take many years. I was hard on myself and long days home alone with Jonah were difficult. I scrutinized my physically perfect son too closely, trying to understand what, besides his developmental lag, made him different. If I wasn't watching him, I was rushing around breathlessly, distracting myself with getting organized. I wanted to keep things around me neat and tidy while inside my emotions roiled. There was no escaping the feeling that my life as a mother had become a tangled mess of loose ends.

Occasionally I invited friends for dinner, happy to share elaborate meals that took hours to prepare. But feeding others became a wounding reminder of my inability to nourish my son with the rudiments of language. There were no ingredients to buy, no recipes to follow.

We'd go to the grocery store, not only to shop, but to learn about Jonah's single greatest passion, food. I'd follow his gaze and talk about the different attributes of what I was holding. "Red apple." "Round cookie." No matter how much I tried or how animated I became, he'd look away. I may as well have been chasing butterflies with a torn net. Most of the time he seemed oblivious, yet his avoidance was purposeful and suspiciously resolute. I didn't want him to look as much as I wanted him to see. He did neither.

The explosion of mental, speech and motor development most parents observe in their babies by their second year bypassed Jonah. He seemed almost too content, unmotivated to move ahead. His physical growth, however, was above average and he was exceptionally beautiful. His expression, which lacked any facial tension, gave him a beatific appearance. Perhaps, I thought, this "Mona Lisa"-like quality was what fueled the misbegotten myth that people with autism are especially beautiful. There was no denying that people gave Jonah greater latitude because of his looks, but I didn't care. Political correctness notwithstanding, I was more than happy to take whatever gave Jonah a leg up.

Still, it became increasingly obvious that I needed time away from the domestic front. I took a part-time job writing advertising copy for Milwaukee's public television station. The office was close to home, the hours were flexible and I spent time with professionals who had more on their minds than child development. Having a legitimate excuse not to be with Jonah every day, all day, helped me enormously. By the time I picked him up from day care, I was energized. Then the real work began.

During that time Michael was finishing his cardiology fellowship and interviewing for jobs. He had offers from hospitals on both coasts, yet was most interested in a position in Detroit. I wasn't excited about moving to the Midwest, and of places to choose, Detroit would have been my least likely pick. But this was no run of the mill job offer. He'd run a lab, work with colleagues he respected, teach and earn a good wage. After much discussion, I agreed to make Motown our home, "but not for more than three years," I made Michael promise.

But the move turned out to be a blessing in disguise. Detroit has since become our home, and more than 23 years later we have no plans to move. The community was warm and welcoming, the lifestyle calm and quiet and services for the disabled were some of the best in the country. Most states offer schooling for the disabled until age 21; in Michigan up to age 26. I adapted to a pace without the push and frenzy of city living. Breathing fresh air and avoiding long commutes didn't hurt either. Naturally there were parts of city living I missed, but I still could, for a doable price, visit pretty much whenever I liked. And being far from family, while hard at times, allowed me to manage our complicated lives as I saw fit. Every town has its pluses and minuses, I discovered, but day-to-day routines, carpooling, making lunches, errand running, look pretty much the same wherever a person lives. I needed hindsight to appreciate this.

Once we arrived in Michigan, I interviewed for a job at the local public television station. I didn't want to work full time or have responsibilities as the managing editor of the station's subscriber magazine but this was the job I was offered. This was an opportunity that made no sense to pass up.

Though my degree was in English literature, I knew I wanted to write. But I'd never had any classes. I wrestled with the idea of spending 40-plus hours each week away from Jonah but taking the position meant getting the training and work experience I lacked. All this plus a salary were not things another degree would provide. Taking the job meant there would be considerable juggling, but Michael and I agreed that it made sense to give it a try.

I thrived on the chaos and the demanding pace of the transition. Michael called me "the blur" as I sped around setting up the apartment, opening accounts and interviewing day care providers in anticipation of my new job. With everything in place, I found going to work a genuine pleasure, much easier than staying home. But I felt guilty each morning when I dropped Jonah at the sitter and left without him responding to my "byes" or blown kisses. I remained focused and organized so that within a year my supervisor allowed me to cut my days at work from five full to three extended days. The arrangement couldn't have been more ideal.

Still there were times I'd look at Jonah's framed picture on my desk and wonder where my priorities were. I'd miss him and rush out of work to find him at daycare sitting alone on the floor or fixating on a toy. While other children gleefully welcomed their parents' arrival or cried because their reappearances reminded them that they had been left behind, Jonah made no connection. He rarely looked up, even when I called his name. Sometimes I'd scoop him up and compensate for his indifference with enough kisses for two. Other times I'd snap the buckle on his car seat feeling crushed and ready to cry.

I desperately wanted to help him, but how? I'd buy bright-colored hard-to-ignore educational toys, but Jonah was more interested in mouthing things than using them purposefully. I knew nothing about teaching and was in the dark about existing therapies. I appeared inept, trying to play teacher; constantly trying to encourage interests but getting nowhere. Schooling or early interventional services weren't even on my radar screen, but clearly Jonah would have qualified. Who knew to ask?

From the moment I was with him until I settled him into his crib at night, I bombarded him with language. I performed a running monologue with words I hoped he'd pick up. Sometimes I'd withhold things I knew he wanted, hoping to motivate some utterance. But Jonah was clear—he would sooner forgo the juice than say the word I was after. Repeating a modeled word earned him whatever he wanted but constantly doing this made life feel like an ongoing Pavlov experiment.

Jonah's interests were few and his attention span limited. Reactive toys, which required pushing a button to trigger noise or a pop-up caught his interest occasionally. Nesting cups and large piece wood puzzles intrigued him as well. But what he sat for best were photograph and picture books, especially if they were read to him in a rhythmic, singsong manner. I'd hold his hand in mine pointing to things, naming them melodically, hopeful that besides learning, he was enjoying our time together. I certainly was.

Jonah loved books with photographs. My favorite was Ruth Krauss' "Leo the Late Bloomer," the story of a tiger cub who watches his animal friends perform antics he is unable to master. Leo worries, as does his father, that he is behind. But Leo's mother expresses her confidence in her son's abilities with a single word, "patience." By the book's end everyone is delighted when Leo proves his mother right. A triumphant Leo catches up just as I hoped Jonah might one day do. If only I'd had his mother's unwavering faith.

Because he was so young, Jonah's delays weren't glaringly obvious. Yet the woman who ran his day-care discreetly expressed her concern. She saw how different he was from the many two and three year olds she had cared for over the years. Her young son attended special education classes and she suggested that I have Jonah evaluated by local school district professionals. I wasn't aware that such assessments existed or that there was any school programming available for such young children. I wondered why my pediatrician, who was concerned about Jonah's development, failed to provide such basic interventional advice.

After being evaluated by a team that included a teacher, psychologist, social worker and speech and physical therapists, Jonah became eligible for an early intervention program. This meant that at age three he would become a student in a Pre-Primary Impaired (PPI) classroom, five, half-days a week. This generic classification is used to protect children from being labeled prematurely. Pre-schoolers with developmental delays, physical disabilities, emotional and behavioral problems were taught with special supports and adjunct therapies. Instead of attending pre-nursery, Jonah became a new inductee into the acronym-rich alphabet soup of special education.

Waiting for the bus with Jonah on that first day of school was bittersweet. He looked like every other youngster in his jean overalls and cartoon character knapsack, but he would board a short yellow bus that publicly declared his special needs. It was at that point that I decided to quit my job and work freelance from home.

We lived in one of the best school districts in the state and besides special pre-nursery schooling, Jonah received physical, occupational and speech therapies. I was grateful to have access to professionals who could teach me what to do with Jonah at home. I also had a chance to meet other parents with similar challenges. But it was Beth, Jonah's teacher, who, to this day, stands out as one of the most remarkable people we met through Jonah. We were in the midst of such a delicate time in our lives, having a child we knew had problems without knowing what they would turn out to be. Beth wasn't much older than I, yet had far more experience with young children. She made me feel safe and reassured that Jonah was being properly taught and cared for.

Beth never judged, tried to be encouraging and positive without being phony or patronizing. Praise, not punishment was her way, and she built on behaviors that others might consider "problematic." When, for example,

Jonah had an issue with spitting, she redirected his behavior by handing him a toothpaste-topped toothbrush. If he were going to spit, she would teach him how to do it appropriately into the sink.

She also taught me how to see Jonah's behavior as his main source of communication, reserve judgment and temper my frustrations. It was apparent how much she loved her students and she set a gold standard that made it tough for the teachers that would follow.

Together we tried to understand Jonah's quirks but also shared stories of progress. The notebook that traveled with Jonah from home to school and back was filled with the little as well as big details that colored his days. But we noticed that if either of us reported a positive change, an almost immediate backslide would follow.

"Jonah's doing much better not running for the tape recorder," Beth would write. The next day his obsessive preoccupation with the device would return, with greater intensity. A note that "he hasn't bitten his wrist in days," meant that the troubling behavior would soon return.

What was strange was how out of touch Jonah seemed. Yet time and time again he seemed to have an uncanny ability to pick up on our observations. We may have joked about the supernatural quality of Jonah's hyper-acuity, but Beth and I grew reluctant to openly applaud Jonah's successes, afraid to jinx his forward strides.

Though numerous professionals at the school saw Jonah regularly, no one, not even Beth, suggested that he might have autism. The disability was less common than it is now, and professionals, if they had any knowledge, were familiar with the stereotypic behaviors associated with disability. Jonah had significant developmental delays and severe speech deficits but he was passive and lacked motivation. Those were not characteristics typically associated with autism at the time.

Jonah getting older didn't make things any more clear. We consulted child psychiatrists, and developmental specialists without a consensus. He was said to have attention deficit disorder, cerebral palsy and perhaps Fragile X. It didn't take expertise to know that the first two diagnoses were incorrect. Fragile X was easily ruled out with a blood test. The question remained – how do you treat something you don't know what to call? And what if there was no treatment at all?

We waited a few more months to see how things evolved and brought him to a psychiatrist, a specialist for children with developmental disabilities. Never sure of what Jonah understood, I avoided talking about him in his presence. The doctor however, didn't feel it was an issue and being easily intimidated, I didn't object. We discussed our concerns and reviewed Jonah's ever-growing pile of reports with him sitting beside me. That acquiescence was a mistake I would never make again.

After finishing his questions, the doctor spent some time alone with Jonah. Ten minutes later he emerged from the office and said," let's talk next week." I wanted immediate answers and wondered what conclusions he could have drawn after spending so little time with him. I would have to wait.

"Your son has autism," he said. "That's impossible," I said defensively. "Jonah smiles, says some words and quiets to my touch." The psychiatrist explained how Jonah's affect had nothing to do with the people around him and that his poor eye contact and inability to respond appropriately for his age were characteristics of the disability. Autism didn't preclude sweet and lovable, the doctor said. That was what Jonah had—he was sure. It was the first time in my life that I fully understood what was meant by the term "a broken heart."

"Will he ever marry?" I stupidly asked, afraid of hearing that Jonah would spend his life alone, without understanding the love and caring I valued in my own marriage. "Highly unlikely," he answered, avoiding my gaze. It was hard to believe—four spoken words and our lives were changed forever.

"Celebrating Jonah"

Before Jonah was born I trained for and ran the New York City marathon. People were impressed that I could condition myself within a year's time to complete the 26.2-mile race. What they failed to appreciate, however, was how much more difficult building up to the first mile was than covering the 26.2-mile distance.

During the first few weeks of training, I spent more time hunched over, trying to catch my breath than I did in motion. At the time it was hard to believe that I would ever be able to run a mile, lct alone 26.2, but before long I could run five, 10 and 15 miles with relative ease. Though I still doubted myself at times, I remained focused. My goal was to complete the course semi-gracefully, and thanks to my perseverance, I did. What I didn't realize at the time was that I had prepared myself for much more than a foot race.

With Jonah's diagnosis I would be running once again, but this time without a finish line. I started by telling family and friends Jonah's official diagnosis. People were compassionate, but I was embarrassed when they admired my strength and ability to handle the situation, as if I had a choice in the matter. Others, confused the word "autistic" with "artistic." If I didn't laugh, I cried.

Explaining the situation was difficult enough, but I realized I would have to be a teacher, introducing friends and family to something they'd never heard of let alone encountered. I tried being positive but at times felt disconnected, as though the painful realities I spoke about had nothing to do with me.

At school, staff and administration questioned the diagnosis, but I knew the doctor was right. All I had to do was sit in on a session of Jonah's speech therapy and watch him avoid eye contact with the therapist for the hour. My marathon finish became an emotional reminder of my ability to be strong and to stay focused. At least, I thought, that was one race I was able to complete.

And while we were glad to finally know what to call Jonah's problem, the information generated new questions. How would our lives evolve when everything would be shaped by Jonah's special needs? What would Jonah's autism mean with respect to having other children? And most importantly, how could we help our son live a meaningful and fulfilling life?

The "experts" we consulted weren't shy about calling Jonah "untreatable" and had no answers about what to expect in the future. They talked a great deal about there being no crystal ball and offered such platitudes as, "you never know," and "time will tell." I called such evasions "non-answer answers." The only concrete advice we got was to get him early educational intervention and pray—things we already knew and did.

We wanted to learn how to navigate this new world we had been thrust into but there weren't many precedents. In previous generations, few children with autism had been raised at home—most spent their lives in institutions. We wanted a roadmap, but would be forced to become pioneers.

We were young, energetic and believed that if we worked hard enough, we could help Jonah overcome his problems and prove the "experts" wrong. Barry Kaufman, after all, author of "Son Rise" had. Kaufman's inspirational memoir chronicles the program he created to successfully cure his son. My mother in-law, a teacher, read and sent us the book wanting us to have the hope none of the professionals would offer.

Kaufman built a cottage industry on his son's cure. Besides books and audiocassettes, he offered guided training at the Option™ Institute, a rustic retreat in the Berkshires. The parent-training brochure we received in the mail was filled with feel good captions such as, "The Gift of a Special Child," "The Parent: The Child's Best

Resource," "The Child as Teacher" and "The Importance of a Loving and Accepting Attitude." Kaufman, a savvy advertising professional, knew his audience and used his success to tap into a niche market.

The more we read, the more we wanted to create an in-home program like Kaufman's. Anxious to get started, we ordered Option™ literature and audiotapes to guide us. The language was empowering and Kaufman's determined, "never-give-up" approach was inspiring. But establishing a program without proper training was like learning to dance from a book—you master the movements but without the heart. We did the best we could given the materials we had to work with but saw we needed more. Even with a $5,000 price tag, there would be several months to wait to begin formal Option™ training.

There was nothing invasive or medically questionable about the Option™ process. At worst, learning to be with Jonah in an alternative way would cost us time and money, small sacrifices considering what Jonah stood to gain. Failing was not something we feared. Standing idly by without at least trying everything humanly possible would have been far worse. We were growing up fast.

For the six months leading up to the training we learned about "non-judgment" and "going with" the child in order to build a trusting relationship. We gave Jonah carte blanche with perseverative behaviors and strange activities hoping this would eliminate his need to be defensive. Whether this approach would increase Jonah's willingness to interact with us became secondary. The belief that we were doing something to help Jonah helped us.

Our Option™ training was scheduled in the early fall. We drove through the forested picture postcard Berkshires and took the incredible autumn beauty as a positive sign of good things to come. Jonah had just celebrated his fourth birthday, and it appeared to be an auspicious time to start a new chapter. I remember sitting in the car and feeling optimistic for the first time in more than a year.

Staff greeted us when we arrived, collected the balance of our tuition and helped settle us in a well-equipped cabin. Despite the modern conveniences, the place, with its pioneer feel, was a reminder of the new terrain we were about to cross.

Implicit in our decision to go to the Option™ Institute was that we believed in the people and what they were doing. Yet I had a hard time shaking my disappointment about the request to pay the tuition balance in a "bank" not "personal" check. Intellectually I accepted that Option™ was a business with expenses that needed to be covered. Yet part of me wanted to believe that something more noble and idealistic drove this operation. I was naive and wanted the caring we would get in the coming days to come without a price tag. But everything, I was slowly discovering, had its costs. There was too much at stake for me to be cynical. I would keep these thoughts to myself and focus instead on getting the most I could from the experience.

The daily schedule was highly structured with morning and afternoon work sessions. Option™ faculty worked one-on-one with Jonah while we observed, analyzed, took notes. Instead of parents, we sat behind a one-way mirror playing scientists.

The room was set up to encourage communication—special floor chairs to foster eye-to-eye contact; toys and books on high shelves that Jonah needed to request or point to. There were no electric sockets or anything dangerous, breakable or off limits. The word "no" was never used. Without an agenda, specific goals or expectations, Jonah could not fail.

Watching Jonah reminded us of our own childhoods. The thought that he had free reign, full control, went against every childrearing book we'd read. It was difficult to temper our intuitive responses, to give up wanting him to do what we thought "should" be done. Still everything seemed natural—from Jonah's unwillingness to respond, to workers respecting his space. Everything was Jonah driven and no matter where you put him or who you put him with, his sessions were "all about Jonah, all the time."

After observing a few times, Mike and I each got to work with him one on one. We were surprised. What the instructors made look easy was remarkably challenging. The energy required was demanding. We were self-conscious about being watched and tried too hard to relax and have fun. I felt like a spectacle and was afraid of what they would see. On the other hand, there was something enormously liberating about an "anything goes" environment. We were not only permitted, but also encouraged to break the rules. Without judgments, nothing was too silly— big dramatic movements—loud noises —whatever it took, we did, to capture Jonah's attention. And if an opportunity to interact meant I handed him puzzle pieces to put back in the box instead of just putting them away myself, that was still one step removed from no interaction at all.

Searching constantly for these windows of opportunity required super-vigilance and endless resources of energy. One could argue that this kind of training supports unrealistic expectations; after all, the world does not organize itself around one human being. But our hope was that in due time, there would be less frustration for Jonah in adapting to the unexpected twists and turns that would occur outside of his room.

Each work session we had with Jonah was followed by a "dialogue.." Basically a faculty member would discuss, in great detail, all that had transpired during the previous session. We enjoyed being indulged, having a captive audience who seemed as interested in discussing Jonah as we were. We felt like part of a team that cared about finding new avenues for reaching Jonah and analyzed ways to build his relatedness. Most of all we were encouraged to think creatively.

Jonah, for example, didn't understand the concept of make believe. Instead of playing doctor, he chewed the rubbery toys in his plastic medical kit. Although the toys satisfied oral needs, we used this interest as an opportunity to teach him what a doctor does. Like him, we would start out by "eating" the stethoscope, seasoning the instrument with imaginary condiments. But once we got him interested, we'd show him how the stethoscope was really used. Though he never initiated what might be called "appropriate" play, he was able, after a few months, to mimic listening to someone's heart. Over and over again we would use whatever interest he had as a bridge to teaching. We had concepts to work with and offered rather than imposed; invited rather than insisting.

The Option™ campus also functioned as a new-age style retreat for individuals wanting to re-evaluate and improve their lives. We were encouraged to join an evening dialogue with the Kaufmans and other attendees, but being turtlenecks and loafers in a sea of tie-dyes and Earth shoes made us reluctant. After finally agreeing to go, we saw that we had more in common with these people than we first assumed. Learning acceptance was the key message that evening.

Kaufman writes, "The difference between a flower and a weed is a judgment," in the preface of his book, "To Love is to be Happy With." Despite being a weed, dandelions, like flowers, have robust color and dramatically change the look of a landscape. Ultimately a person chooses whether or not to see a disability as a "weed" that needs eliminating or "a flower-like" variant of the normal world. Acceptance extended beyond the Jonah world, and meant being flexible, expanding our views beyond what was expected.

During our stay we were also introduced to Raun, Kaufman's cured son and the subject of "Son-Rise." We scrutinized the handsome, friendly teenager who spoke and smiled easily with no trace of residual autism. I wasn't sure if he was supposed to inspire us or was simply a part of the Option™ script, but I pitied him, having to talk to a parade of ogling strangers, just because he was normal.

We wrapped up the week feeling exhausted and inspired, good about what we had learned, intimidated by all that we would have to do. Setting up a program such as this would require an enormous effort and many more hands than we had. The question was where to begin.

Besides constructing the kind of workroom we had seen at Option™, I would need to recruit a team of helpers. Ideally the one-on-one program would run seven days a week. With 16-hour days to fill I would need lots of manpower. I posted ads in college papers, community houses, recreation centers, churches and synagogues. I compiled publicity material, spoke at high schools and met with college professors. So little was known about autism, I told them. No one teaching method was proven to work and our program was an innovative opportunity for independent study. Why not allow psychology, social work and special education students to try this experimental program? Maybe they would have breakthroughs with a child that doctors called "untreatable."

I would also have to handle the training piece of the program. Once we had people to teach, I would demonstrate for and observe them, help them enjoy and optimize their time with Jonah. I'd tell them what a difference they could make, organize schedules, review and record notes and lead semi-monthly meetings with staff. The program, which we called "Celebrating Jonah," would become my new full-time job.

I talked a lot about acceptance and followed the tenets of the Option™ philosophy. But looking back, whether we admitted it at the time or not, the hope was that we would be able to duplicate the Kaufman's' magic and cure our son. Were we being dishonest? Had we missed the point? Acceptance, we would discover, was a process, one that would take far more than just a few days of training. Without realizing it at the time, we'd taken the first of many baby steps.

Jonah's "Angels"

While most of my friends with four-year olds were having second or third babies, I was about to give birth to a program. If life had followed a different course I too would have probably been growing our family, but Jonah's needs dominated our lives. Though it was counterintuitive, we did what child rearing books cautioned against—made Jonah and his program the focus of our lives.

No one questioned our single-mindedness about the program. Nothing could shake our belief in what we were doing. We were bound to and by Jonah—and felt lucky that our priorities were in sync. We'd seen the push and pull of adversity, how it destroyed marriages and left families in ruins. In our case, the problems deepened our bond. That is not to say that Mike and I did not argue—we did—mostly about Jonah. But no matter how heated our disagreements became, we never lost sight of our common goal—helping our child.

At times the intense preoccupation with what we were doing made life feel claustrophobic. I had no problem talking openly and honestly with Michael yet I wanted to share things with someone who could understand my life without living under the same roof. Kate was that person. She'd also gone through Option™ training and ran an in-home program for her young son with autism. Fortunately for me, she lived just a few miles away.

Autism has a language of its own and, to speak it correctly, one must know it intimately. Both of us did. We had similar educational backgrounds, the street savvy to navigate the bureaucracies of the special needs world and families we put first.

Unlike Jonah, Kate's son was independent, able to roam freely, busy himself contentedly for hours at a time. As different as our children were, however, we faced many of the same challenges; recruiting and keeping help; finding appropriate activities for endless days and the inevitable fears associated with an uncertain future.

We became close and turned to one another for honest answers to tough questions. Who, after all, could I relate to more than someone who was living my life? Though they had nothing to do with one another, our sons connected us and created an easy intimacy that, in some cases, trumped years of friendship I had with others. The relationship also accommodated our enormous family demands and thrived without much tending.

Together we advocated for our children but also told each other the truth. There was no shortage of conflicted feelings and worries we shared and that strengthened our unique bond.

From her I learned the extraordinary value of having a friend who walks the same road. For this reason, years later when friends fell ill or faced a difficult situation, I encouraged them to find a friend dealing with similar issues. The person best able to understand what you go through is someone else going through the same thing.

Kate was the only person who understood my fantasy about wanting to run away or my thoughts about Jonah running out after "mistakenly" leaving the door open. She shared her worries about her non-verbal son being kidnapped, and unable to tell the abductor where he lived, never be returned. Only she understood what I meant when I said our fears were also half-wishes. That we loved and were devoted to our sons was a given, but there was no denying that there were days both of us wished for a way out. We learned from each other and took turns being hard on ourselves.

Having help, for example, was difficult for me. I thought that I should be able to do everything on my own. If Option's™ message was about acceptance, then I seemed to have missed the point when it came to myself. The program would not—could not—work unless I stopped seeing help as a negative, something I needed because of my own shortcomings. Watching Kate manage her team of helpers allowed me to see how delegating more to others enhanced rather than diminished what she was trying to accomplish. Acknowledging this was the beginning; getting comfortable with the idea took much longer.

When I finally decided to recruit the help I obviously needed, I threw my net wide. Most applicants turned out to be college students, young idealists who liked that the program was off the beaten track. They were challenged by the mainstream view that autism was "untreatable" and recognized the strength of individuality. Because of their youth, they possessed the 3Es, "Energy, Enthusiasm and Excitement" we sought.

During initial interviews we were upbeat and positive, trying hard to convey the worthiness of what we were doing. We asked applicants for at least one semester's commitment and in return arranged for them to get independent study credits. I promised that they would grow personally from the experience—find stores of patience they never knew they had; learn to be in a relationship that appeared to be all give; and discover how, with a little imagination, they could transform the mundane into the magical.

At first, no one seemed to mind making a semester-long commitment. But that was before they saw how all consuming the work could be. This was no babysitting job—and sustaining the level of energy Jonah required was exhausting. Some left soon after they started, others lasted a few weeks.

We were partly to blame. We were selling a program and worked hard to make spending time with Jonah look easy. We modeled play sessions by using favorite toys, routines and perseverations in a predictable, nearly scripted style. Our handouts painted a picture of a sweet docile boy and failed to include one teacher's description of Jonah as "a wolf in sheep's clothing." We were marketing a program, wanting newcomers to focus on Jonah's strengths and not his challenging behaviors. We weren't being dishonest; we just avoided the information that might send people running.

Jonah also had a difficult time with strangers. When newcomers were introduced he would refuse eye contact, pull hair, throw toys and eyeglasses, mess his diaper repeatedly and fight all attempts to change him. He'd bite his wrist forcefully, a gesture that expressed defiance, frustration and anxiety. Unable to communicate, new people would quickly learn that his behavior said everything.

I wasn't surprised that new recruits were overwhelmed and intimidated. I apologized, made excuses, told them what they were seeing wasn't because of anything that they did. I wanted them to like Jonah. But I had been selling them an incomplete bill of goods and they were disappointed when things were not as straightforward as they expected. Projecting my own fears and discomforts about his behavior turned out to be counterproductive.

So I changed my approach, radically. Instead of neat and tidy, I presented the messy facts. I went to the opposite extreme, warning candidates to be careful that Jonah might bite them when he was picked up. It was not uncommon for Jonah to grab and pull shiny earrings and loose hair. "Avoid jewelry and wear your hair back," I cautioned. *"Be yourselves,"* I encouraged, and "react naturally." Jonah was keenly aware of posturing and false praise. He did not like phoniness. With that information it was hard for people not to appreciate the enormous challenge of engaging an uninterested, resistive, non-verbal child.

Those who made it through Jonah's initiation period generally stayed on. Sometimes after weeks of coming regularly relationships developed. On occasion there were breakthrough moments—periods of lucidity when Jonah seemed to get it or was willing to be engaged. Though these times came relatively infrequently, they made the seemingly difficult hours seem worthwhile. Still, there were long stretches when Jonah tuned people out and resisted interaction. Sometimes these young students lacked the maturity and patience necessary to see the big picture and wanted to move on before the semester was over. Departures made me panic. I was terrified of being left alone to care for Jonah.

I considered paying helpers but didn't want to taint the idealism I thought should fuel the program. But growing personally and watching Jonah develop, did not seem to be enough for most. The constant staff turnover sounded an alarm bell that made me realistic. I was aware that once I put money on the table, there would be no turning back. But I needed help as much as the helpers needed to earn and with that I added bookkeeper to my evolving roster of program related jobs.

Good coverage was when there were five to eight people coming on a regular basis. With colleges on break, summer was the easiest time to find help, but it was also the time Jonah was home most. All year long our front entry became a revolving door. Most who came to help entered our lives as strangers. Yet within a short span of time they would know our lives intimately. There wasn't a time of day that was off limits, so that they came early, left late, ate at our dinner table, drove our cars and used our belongings. When someone was in a bad mood I treaded lightly; when they wanted to talk I became their confidant; when they had a problem I became a counselor. Relationships, money and school issues— all topics were fair game and, whether I liked it or not, I had to be a compassionate listener. I needed them too much to risk losing them.

Although I felt indebted to these workers for their help, I also felt lacking for not being able to care for Jonah alone. I was supposed to be the person in charge, yet I sometimes put the needs of helpers before my own just so that they would keep coming. I was frustrated by my lack of solitude. I was expected to be upbeat and welcoming but on tough days I felt like a complete phony. I was saying "yes" when I wanted to say "no," calling myself a "help whore" because I was willing to sell my soul just to retain staff.

Our privacy would be further compromised when we realized that we also needed a constant back up for me. While I was busy debriefing staff about their sessions with Jonah, he would sit or run around unsupervised. With Jonah on the loose, feedback sessions were constantly being interrupted. It was hard not to appreciate the irony. We needed someone to care for Jonah while I cared for his help.

I was uncomfortable with the idea of having someone live-in, but once again, the necessity was undeniable. These were the times I missed not having family living close by.

I advertised for someone who spoke English, didn't smoke and had references. It seemed reasonable and yet I had a parade of interviews that were both laughable and frightening. An array of women, some who had never lived with running water indoors came to our door. After several weeks of fruitless interviews, I finally hired a woman who supposedly understood English. She was nice, happy doing housework, and nodded yes no matter what question was asked. No matter how many times I showed her, she couldn't get the hang of being with Jonah, even for a few minutes. Interestingly, my inability to communicate with her allowed me to appreciate Jonah's inability to convey his wants to us. Nice as she was, I let her go.

I was disheartened by all the coming and goings of people, and my mother, trying to reassure me, would remind me that I only "needed one." She was right. Dora came to us through a friend's housekeeper, a single mom who wanted to earn money for her children back home in the Philippines. Having suffered her own hardships before coming to America, she innately understood the meaning of struggle, and from early on, rallied to help me whenever she could. She was compassionate, soft-spoken, knew when to get involved and when to disappear. She became the prototype of the people we would come to call "Jonah's Angels," exceptional people who, over time, became adopted members of our extended family. She was truly a godsend.

But she was one of many. We were blessed with a long list of people who came into our lives because of Jonah, among them Carly, a beautiful, gentle soul with a Disney view of the world. If autism was the villain, she wanted to be the hero. She lit up a room with her positive energy and described her initial meeting with Jonah as "love at first sight." It didn't take long to see that the feeling was mutual.

Three or more times a week she worked one-on-one with Jonah, always blending learning with fun and affection. Jonah's autism was not something limiting to Carly—it gave her reason to give and love him more. She was the "can do" kind of person who tried to figure out ways to improve things that already seemed good enough. If Jonah mastered a 12-piece puzzle she encouraged him to try 20, and then 25. She sat beside him, as he moved ahead, step by minuscule step.

Carly set a gold standard, always claiming that she got as much as she gave. But she also loved being a part of our family picture. With her talents in music and athletics she could have pursued a wide variety of careers yet chose to teach children with autism. She has won awards as a gifted teacher and to this day she credits Jonah for being her inspiration.

Debra, another angel, arrived a few months after Carly. This small town girl's tough-as-nails exterior belied her soft heart, especially when it came to the little brother she never had. I thought of her as my best stand-in, yet unlike me, she never became overwhelmed. She was comfortable taking Jonah everywhere and loved championing his rights, especially when people gave her a hard time about his behavior.

Determined to help Jonah overcome gross motor delays, she took him to an indoor pool several times a week, even during the coldest winter months. Nothing fazed her. It was because of her that Jonah learned to swim. It remains one of the few recreational activities he still enjoys today.

Dora, Carly and Debra are people who say that Jonah changed their lives in meaningful ways. We feel the same way about them. Though they were young, perhaps lacking the gravitas of adulthood, they were indispensable. Without them, we would never have been able to manage. To them I will always be indebted and grateful.

Though Michael was less involved with the helpers because of his long work hours, he still valued their enormous contributions. Together we took a team approach and scheduled regular monthly meetings to review progress, trends, ideas, innovations or suggestions. There were the usual personality clashes, but Mike and I anchored the meetings, trying to make them as productive as possible. The greatest source of debate was Jonah's progress.

People were naturally eager to report forward strides but Michael, ever the scientist, wouldn't accept an accomplishment as a step forward unless there was consistency and reproducibility. People were annoyed by his skepticism. The situation was reminiscent of the new mother who calls her baby's expression a "smile" only to have someone say "it was just gas." Because of this I was often called upon to play the role of peacemaker.

I was caught in the middle, wanting to support Michael, yet fearful of alienating staff. He left early each morning and came home late in the evening without understanding how desperately dependent I was on these people. He focused on refining the program while my main concern was keeping it afloat. It was difficult for him to see that besides helping Jonah, these people allowed me to breathe.

We spent the major part of a year doing the program exclusively at home, but between the stresses generated by staff and going stir crazy from spending so much time in the basement teaching and observing, I thought about sending Jonah to school part-time. I rationalized that by attending the nearby autism school program he would have more opportunity to socialize with peers and get the speech, physical and occupational therapies he needed. Besides riding the bus with neighborhood children he would be spending time with peers who might serve as role models.

This arrangement fell outside the usual parameters of Option™ but my friend Kate had drawn the same conclusion. She decided to send her son to school for identical reasons. We would still be dependent on volunteers, but thankfully, less so.

With Jonah at school part of each day, things became more structured and felt like they were falling into place. We were always searching for alternative ways to do and improve things. But of all the difficulties generated by doing the in-home program, nothing hit harder than losing staff. No matter who left, I'd feel personally abandoned. Intellectually, I accepted that people moved on. But I saw these helpers as Jonah's friends, the only ones mature enough to compensate for his inability to give. On their way out the door they would always promise to visit and sometimes they did. But invariably within a few months they'd disappear, never to be seen or heard from again.

Jonah's birthdays were especially difficult – bittersweet celebrations of joy laced with loss, a reminder of time's passage and all the people who had come and gone. Instead of feeling excited about Jonah's forward strides we were reminded of how much wider the developmental gap was becoming. Jonah was indifferent to the people and hubbub generated in his honor and needed to be held back from lunging at his homemade Big Bird cake. We sang "Happy Birthday," took photos, opened gifts with smiles and a sense of celebration. But it hurt when I looked around the room fully aware that many of the guests would probably be gone by his next birthday. That's how it was —they came and went. I was grateful Jonah did not understand what was clear to me—that his life would be filled people who cared about him, but for a limited time only. At least he could count on us. We would be there for him forever.

A Bargain with G-d

My 35th birthday came and went with an increasing sense that Jonah was destined to be an only child. Michael and I discussed having a family before getting married, but understood, even in our youthful naiveté, the difference between two needy and four easygoing children. We'd decided then that the size of our clan would be determined by the needs of each family member as they came along. Jonah was already the work of a brood and without a crystal ball, we weren't sure we could handle any more unexpected challenges.

With all that I was shouldering, Michael felt I should have the final say about having more children. He claimed to be content with the status quo, never pressuring me to get on with growing our family. I appreciated his patience and generosity, traits that I once dreamed we would pass on to children. But fear outweighed my longing. Without prenatal tests to screen for autism, I was too terrified to take the plunge.

We consulted a geneticist who after drawing our blood and taking detailed family histories ruled out Fragile X, a syndrome with similar features to autism. Still there were no ironclad answers about future children. I wanted autism to be like lightening that never struck twice in the same place. I wanted to believe that life's heartache was portion-controlled and we'd already gotten our helping. The doctor we consulted, however, was not in the business of indulging magical thinking. He told us that subsequent pregnancies would be a high stakes gamble with a one in four chance of a repeat Jonah situation.

To reduce those odds, he recommended using a sperm or egg donor to conceive. Petri dish and test tube reproduction were making headlines at the time and seemed more like science fiction than conception alternatives. The last thing our lives needed at that point was more of the unusual. If we were to roll the childbearing dice again, we decided, we would do it the old fashioned way.

That I was realistic about what we were up against in having another child was a step in the right direction. Yet I felt guilty, wondering if I had done or neglected to do something to cause Jonah's autism. Friends, many of them medical professionals, assured me that things happened in spite of what I did—I wasn't as powerful as I thought. Knowing these feelings were textbook for parents of disabled children however did little to allay their impact. I needed to let go. Easier said than done.

I also felt wanting another child so desperately was an indirect diminishment of Jonah. Shouldn't he have been enough? The more I struggled to free myself from these emotions, the more entangled they became. I needed to talk to someone, a professional who could help me unravel the web that became increasingly difficult to escape.

The therapist I saw was fatherly, quietly patient—a nice counterpoint to my obsessive bundle of nerves. He was reasoned when I was frantic and helped steady the mirror so I could examine a variety of issues which interfered with my life. Though he had no firsthand experience with autism, he understood Jonah's impact and why, the wind had been taken out of my childbearing sail. My feelings and fears made sense. Because of Jonah's autism, my situation would not be easy to resolve. Therapy could take years and the alarm on my biological clock was loud and insistent.

My inner distractions impacted Jonah's home schooling as well. "Acceptance" may have been Option's™ maxim, yet it became harder for the people working with Jonah to sustain the required level of energy without seeing measurable results. Staff turnover continued to be a problem as was Jonah's often changing and unpredictable needs. His developmental gap continued to widen, yet Michael and I tried to remain positive. We talked "progress" though we were content to stave off regression. Staff did what they preferred to do in the room rather than what was needed and interactions, once the lifeblood of the program, became formulaic and lost momentum.

Wanting to retain staff, I allowed more and more of the work with Jonah to be taken outside the room. Helpers reasoned that "he needed fresh air; that being in the room so many hours each day prevented him from experiencing the real world." I was in no position to debate.

Given all that was going on it seemed almost irresponsible to consider adding another family member to the mix. But I told myself I wouldn't be the first woman on the planet raising a family with a child who had autism. There would be unusual challenges, but I had a solid support system and was trying to get a better handle on my life. Not only would having another child be the fulfillment of a personal dream, but also it would be, I believed, the best thing for our family.

"G-d gives you what you can handle," was the coined response I often heard when people learned of Jonah's autism. I resented the comment, a platitude meant as an answer for the unexplainable. Yet when I became pregnant, I wanted those words to be true. If I was getting another crack at motherhood, I hoped G-d would see how much we had to handle and cut us some slack. Pregnancy books lacked chapters on "negotiating deals with G-d," so I peppered my prayers with private promises that "if I had a normal baby. . . then . . . ." I would promise anything in order to have a child that might some day call me "mom."

Despite my fears I took the plunge. We kept my pregnancy under wraps for as long as we could, quietly absorbing our new reality. Our main concern was the baby's health, though it wasn't clear what we would do with prenatal testing information. We went ahead and signed a pile of release forms for a partial glimpse into our future. I would undergo Chorionic villus sampling (CVS), a new, relatively low-risk procedure that provided similar genetic information as amniocentesis, but at a much earlier stage in the pregnancy.

The test, which is done in the tenth week of pregnancy, involves a needle extraction of cells while having an ultrasound, something I'd never had before. Lying on the table in a darkened room, grainy shadows of black and white appeared on the illuminated screen. I was tense and emotional, afraid of what I might see. The technician outlined a kidney bean shape with a point that flashed rhythmically. "That's the baby's heart," she said. Enthralling as it was to see our legume-sized child, we left the hospital terrified that a problem might be discovered. I had witnessed life on that screen, something I could never imagine ending if G-d forbid, the news was bad. Fortunately that was not the case— the news was good—I was carrying Jonah's little brother who, at least genetically, appeared to be fine.

Though I'd seen my gynecologist for annual checkups since Jonah's birth six years earlier, I was surprised by how obstetric visits had changed. Women in the waiting area talked about their babies in the here and now, casually referring to them by sex and name, leaving few surprises for delivery day. Weren't they afraid of the evil eye? I wasn't very forthcoming, but listened closely and smiled.

By the fifth month my body made clear that I was more than just putting on a few pounds. Family and friends were thrilled by our announcement, but this time when they asked if I wanted a boy or a girl I said "healthy" with new conviction. There were days that I worried, but between the demands of Jonah and day-to-day life, there was plenty to distract me. Having a professional to talk to also helped. Still during darker moments I'd ask Michael what we would do if the new baby had autism?

"We'll build another room," he'd say referring to the Option™ style workroom we'd built for Jonah. Michael had a gift for lightening the mood when I fretted and I tried to do the same for him. Like many couples, we'd found a balance alternating roles of needing and giving support. But knowing I had someone I could depend on made me think of Jonah's yet to be born younger brother. Who would he have to lean on when we were no longer around? He would need a partner, more than a spouse, ideally someone who was equally vested in Jonah. Another sibling would fit the criteria but I was getting ahead of myself. I was in the throes of a second pregnancy, dealing with so many unknowns, thinking of having a third child. I was mapping out a future using reason and logic, forgetting the joke, "What makes God laugh? Plans."

The pregnancy generated a positive energy in the household. It was wonderful just to be able to think about a future with a child that could say, "I love you." We kept Jonah's life on an even keel and though we taught him to point to my belly when I asked, "Where is the baby?" it was obvious he had no understanding of what was happening.

I was due in early spring, a few months before summer vacation. People worried how we would manage once Jonah was home full-time, but we had a good support system with Dora, Carly and Debra around. Beyond that, there were no assurances I could offer. Like us, everyone would have to grow accustomed to rolling with the punches.

My mother-in-law, our family's unofficial autism scout, sent us an article about a new residential school for children with autism. Was she suggesting that we send Jonah away? The Boston Higashi School was an American satellite of a longstanding, highly regarded Japanese program. "Read the books," my mother-in-law wrote in the note she enclosed with the three volumes written by the school's founder, Kito Kitahara.

Since Jonah's birth we'd never made any inquiries about residential schools. Jonah was so young and as difficult as things sometimes became, we always seemed to manage. Besides, images of abuses uncovered in such places haunted us and made considering such a place impossible.

"Just visit," both sets of grandparents urged. Jonah, after all was getting every kind of help imaginable yet wasn't making much progress. They were well intentioned and wanted the best for all of us. They genuinely believed that Jonah might do better elsewhere. They pointed to Higashi's success in helping the most intractable children become toilet trained, something we hadn't even begun working on with Jonah. He was over six years old and still in diapers

We read and reread the school literature with a skeptic's eye. It didn't matter that a Harvard physician was a school consultant. Or that the school's focus on daily living skills made sense; or that they avoided using medication to manage behavior; or that they went outside the box, employing unicycles and stilts to challenge and strengthen focusing abilities. I dug in my heels and refused to consider a residential school.

But after many months of heated conversation we decided to look at the school, but only as part of a weekend getaway. I was uneasy, knowing that so many unexpected twists and turns in our lives had begun in this unsuspecting way. Even if I fell in love with the school, I told Michael, Jonah wasn't going unless we went with him.

It was summer, and the school was having its annual summer celebration, the carnival-like event which marked the beginning of the school's summer break. The atmosphere was festive; the environment clean and cheery. Colorful drawings lined the school hallways and people, students as well as parents and staff, appeared relaxed and happy. Many of the families had moved to the Boston area, just for access to the school. They were encouraging, and gave the school high marks for teaching their children what others were never able to before.

Students included a three-year old from London as well as a 21-year old who commuted daily from Rhode Island. Some children were verbal and independent, others were not. Everyone seemed to be on their best behavior, with lines of uniformed youngsters coming and going to designated areas. There was a sense of structure and organization, but I refused to act too interested. I was defensive, determined to find fault with the place. There was no way I would consider letting Jonah go.

After we returned home I mentally filed the Higashi information away, hopeful that I would never again have to revisit the school. As hard as things were, I was crazy about our little boy and wanted him cared for by me. Call it blind devotion, but I didn't care. Still, imagining what it would be like not to have to be a constant and super-vigilant caregiver was seductive. Admittedly, on difficult days I would think, "Sign him up and run like the wind." And while the temptation was great, the guilt was greater. I wasn't ready for such a radical change and was determined to work harder than ever to prove that Jonah could make progress while living at home.

The last trimester of my pregnancy passed quickly and culminated in the arrival of Jonah's little brother, David

Samuel. Naming him was straightforward, both of my parents had a brother David who perished in concentration camps. We chose the name Samuel because the biblical figure had a mother with the same Hebrew name as mine, Chana. But we had more than just a name in common. I, like she, had cried and prayed for the birth of a child. Samuel means "God heard" and indeed he had, in both her case and mine.

It was a Cadillac delivery thanks to an epidural, something I still regret not having had with Jonah. After his birth I was clear headed and held my baby with a sense of motherly confidence I'd lacked before. There had been moments of fetal distress, not that unusual we were told; yet it was frighteningly reminiscent of what had happened with Jonah. Though I scrutinized David for the first few months, intuitively I knew he was fine. And he was. He ate and slept well, had a sweet disposition, and in most respects was a dream baby. With his birth, a lifetime fantasy had been realized. I'd officially become a mother of "kids," someone who had a legitimate reason for replacing her Volvo sedan with a much longed for minivan.

Caring for David may have been relatively easy, there was still much more going on at home. I had help, yet was running around full-time, at least now with a hopeful and happy kick in my step. But there was a price. With only so many hours in the day and two young children needing attention I was torn. If I needed a reason to feel guilty, I had one. With David's birth, Jonah's days of exclusivity were over.

School Days

David's birth in early spring marked the start of new beginnings. Our already hectic lives picked up pace, and though we were bleary eyed much of the time, we became more adept at juggling. Our focus remained on Jonah and how to help him move forward. His "autistically impaired" (AI) classroom was housed in our district elementary school which meant he could eat lunch and play with neighborhood children during recess. We believed school would provide what we could not at home—an environment of social peers, as well as speech, physical and occupational therapies. Yet being in a classroom with non-communicative children didn't provide many opportunities for him to interact. We talked about him being "included" in a regular education kindergarten, and to our surprise, the administration said "yes."

Once referred to as mainstreaming, inclusion was considered cutting edge. Students with autism spent time with regular education peers who learned about disabilities and helping others. In Jonah's case however, things weren't quite that straightforward. Jonah's kindergarten teacher tried, with the help of an aide, to make him part of the group but instead of playing with others, he spent most of his time dumping toys, flipping pages of books or running off to be pushed on a swing. Sometimes he'd sit for circle or story time, but he was mostly on his own, indifferent to what was going on around him. He marched alongside this group of five and six year olds, but clearly was out of step.

Wearing diapers, especially soiled ones, didn't help. They made him a target for teasing and became a symbol of how out of sync he was. As with most things Jonah didn't care what others thought but I'd decided that the more time we let go by, the harder he would be to toilet train. I was ready to put all our energy into teaching him how to use the bathroom.

To create an agenda ran counter to Option™ thinking, but I didn't care. I'd been watching for the toilet training readiness signs everyone assured me Jonah would eventually demonstrate, but he never did. I felt like we might have waited too long. We'd have double the work, first helping him unlearn old patterns before introducing him to better alternatives. Option™ had inspired us, given us direction and helped us cultivate great connections and

I was grateful for all that I had learned. But I was ready to declare my independence. There needed to be some rules and guidelines. This kind of thinking was a departure for me; a signal that I was beginning to trust my judgment about what was best for Jonah.

None of us had any illusions about the challenge we were taking on. To begin with, Jonah didn't know how to make sense of his bodily sensations and functions. Toilet training would require double the vigilance on our part and at least some cooperation from Jonah. That was a tall order. Jonah's indifference about wearing diapers meant that he had no impetus to change. Additionally there was almost nothing he cared enough about to motivate him. He had his likes and dislikes, but would sooner abandon things he wanted than be coaxed into doing or trying something new. Food and toys were short-lived lures, and praise, never moved him. Finding something that would interest and excite him over the long term would be a major challenge.

Spin and cause effect toys were attractive but old hat. We needed something portable, replaceable and not too messy. Anything Disney was appealing—characters, books, toys, puzzles and tapes. Noise, especially shrill high-pitched or deep angry sounds excited him. He needed a double lure, something that would pique his interest visually and auditorily. We found a Disney-themed touch-and-talk computer that was designed to teach the ABC's. Press a letter, and Mickey Mouse's voice would go into a high-pitched spiel. We called the battery-run charm the "Mickey Toy," and with that and a warehouse club-sized bottle of ibuprofen, we were in business.

We took him out of school before summer break and, with the beginning of warmer weather, dressed him in underwear and t-shirts. The spring term was about to end at local colleges and Jonah's best staff would be available to work full time.

Jonah loved the Mickey Toy and wanted it badly, but had a hard time understanding why he couldn't have it all the time. Part of the plan was frustrating him but not to the point of turning him off, a fine line not easily negotiated. For Jonah to get the toy, he needed to connect his bodily sensations to the bathroom. How does one explain such an abstract concept to a nonverbal child? Consequently there were a disproportionate number of errors for every trial. Still we remained determined and persevered.

After a few weeks of wearing underpants and being housebound Jonah sensed something was up. He became a master at withholding —allowing us to follow him closely sometimes for up to three days without soiling himself. He would find the exact moment when no one was looking to have private "accidents." We were mystified. If he was truly as oblivious as he seemed, how could he do, or in this case *not do,* something so purposefully.

This was the ongoing Jonah conundrum. So many times we had looked at him sure that he understood more than he let on—that he had some deep knowledge that he simply was unable to share. People who knew Jonah well also had that feeling, believing like us, that his big brown eyes were making silent sense of the world. It wasn't that he had special gifts in math or drawing, but that at times, things seemed to register. He'd be responsive-— in the here and now with the people he was with, but only fleetingly. Other days he seemed gone, lost in his private domain, laughing at things going on inside his head. He would be so out of touch at times, that he'd persist in drinking from the same empty cup over and over again. It was sweetly amusing on one level, heartbreaking on another.

Nothing we taught Jonah was learned or generalized easily. So that even if he was successful using the toilet at home, he didn't understand that the same rules applied in other environments. Almost everything he seemed to learn and understand was underscored by inconsistency. Toilet training was especially challenging. We'd kick ourselves about "misses" and had to acknowledge that his few successes were just a matter of our getting him to the toilet in time. To prevent accidents we took him to the bathroom before we left the house and once again, as soon as we returned. We logged how much Jonah took in and put out and photographed his Mickey Toy, trophy style, atop the toilet. No one's digestive system or "tush", I joked, deserved that level of scrutiny.

Everything toileting-related was a matter of prompting on our part, so that left to his own devices, Jonah, it may have appeared, accomplished *nothing* over the summer. But he had. Besides gleaning an understanding, albeit a disorganized one, of what bathrooms were for, we had discovered a behavior pattern.

Prior to toileting accidents Jonah would become hyperactive, turn away from us and stiffen his legs. If we caught the clues early enough we might be more successful. But to build on this, he needed more time at home. Many of the summer helpers had already returned to college and David was beginning to wake from his infantile oblivion. I wasn't prepared to have Jonah home full-time and though I felt guilty, sent him back to school, but this time in underpants. Surely his teachers should have been able to pick up where we left off, especially since toileting is such a fundamental life skill. But if we sent him to school without diapers we were told, he would no longer be allowed to spend time in the regular education classroom. I didn't really care; Jonah hadn't benefited that much from the experience anyway. I met with his teachers before school began, wrote out the details of all we'd accomplished that summer and made clear that Jonah's number one educational goal for that year had to be toilet training. I also offered to visit the classroom often to lend a hand.

I sent a notebook and Jonah's Mickey Toy to school daily, hoping to hear about the day's activities in addition to bathroom updates. This would allow me to *talk* to Jonah about projects he brought home or things he did at school. Instead of providing valuable information, the notebook became a toileting log, with messages about "BMs in the a.m." or "urine in the p.m." "All toileting news, all the time," became the running joke among us at home.

Each time I went to school to help out, I'd find Jonah sitting alone, unsupervised. When he'd come home with a bag full of soiled pants and a note to send more clothes and perhaps some diapers, I was furious. No one kept the close eye on him that he needed. I knew that without that and lots of encouragement from staff, his hours at school would be a toileting fiasco. I kept reminding everyone that they had to watch for his *signs*, yet received a note from his teacher right before the Thanksgiving break that said, "he's not ready." I knew that kind of thinking would keep Jonah in diapers indefinitely. The teacher refused to accept that he had been making slow, but steady progress all summer.

Jonah's return to school after our Herculean effort that summer, marked the beginning of a major backslide. All we'd had accomplished with Jonah was disregarded. The teacher wanted him back in diapers but I refused. I was angry but stood my ground without being adversarial. Jonah would not be compromised for the sake of the teacher's convenience.

Up until that point I had been the deferring negotiator, the one who wanted to make everyone happy, sometimes at our expense. I treated every school meeting as a gift, impressed that a room full of professionals would spend so much time talking about my son. But I felt the school staff should have been able to pick up where we left off. We had initiated this project and committed five 24/7 months to getting his toilet training off the ground. They had him a few hours a day, rarely for a full week at a time, and didn't want to be bothered with bathroom accidents. I understood how they felt yet no matter how much they tried to sway me; my answer to their request that he wear a diaper to school was "absolutely no."

It was a transitional time for me personally. With David's birth I became more confident in my mothering abilities. I was managing two children, watching the miracle of David's normalcy emerge. With Jonah, I had never been able to gauge whether what I was doing was right or wrong and the sense of painful failure seemed to be never-ending. David, by contrast, was an unfurling book, with new chapters added minute by minute. It was exciting to watch this little person develop, yet it also highlighted how far behind his brother continued to fall.

I was also beginning to appreciate my power as an advocate. Even without a degree in teaching or psychology, I began to see that I was the Jonah expert, the one who could, besides adding heart, add substance to any conversation about him.

This changed the nature of Jonah's annual Individualized Education Plans (IEPs), which are supposed to map out the educational goals for each special education student. In the early days I couldn't believe that a room filled with paid professionals devoted time to customizing an educational program for Jonah. But the enchantment wore thin once I realized the meetings were a means to an end, a formality aimed at securing a signature on a formal legal document.

We struggled with toileting for the next two years during which time I was pregnant with and gave birth to Jonah and David's younger sister, Ruth. The year Jonah turned nine Michael and I sat in the school conference room amazed by how thick and heavy Jonah's file had become. A variety of tests, assessments, inventories, had been administered, mainly to get a handle on Jonah's intellectual and functional progress. I looked around at the motley assortment of professionals, anticipating what we would hear. These people spent more time going to meetings, filling out reports, attending special education symposiums and enjoying school breaks, than sharing face time with any of the students in Jonah's program. How ironic that this crew of conference and meeting comers and goers were in charge of a group of children who needed consistency. It made me question how well could they possibly know Jonah. I didn't expect any major surprises given that I was at the school often, checking in, following up and observing. This particular IEP, however, would be different.

The district's special education administrator barely knew Jonah. She sat stiffly at the large conference table, her eyeglasses cocked at the tip of her nose, overseeing the group in a judge like manner. The social worker reviewed her copious notes looking up periodically to check for questions while the speech therapist's color coordinated powder blue outfit along with her perfectly manicured nails said a great deal about her remoteness with the children. The occupational and physical therapists read long, boring evaluations while Jonah's overworked and underpaid aide spoke lovingly about what a great kid he was. Jonah's teacher spoke in vagaries, her fake cheeriness completely turning me off and making me want to punch something. Being angry went with the territory—these professionals, in my opinion, should have been able to do more to help Jonah. Some were genuine, well-intentioned individuals who wished they could. I appreciated their efforts. Others, however, were just clocking in.

I was also upset that my child was not like others in the adjacent rooms, whose parents got to attend parent-teacher conferences for regular education students. I was tethered to a world of *supports* with nothing substantive to show for it. I questioned how the big special education budgets were being spent. I could have easily digressed into an angry tirade. But Michael calmed me down and as usual, mediated with grace and a smile.

The psychologist couldn't make the meeting so the social worker was asked to present her findings. We listened as she told us that Jonah functioned at the developmental range of six to 18 months with an IQ that numerically, wasn't much higher. I was not surprised. How could they accurately assess an unresponsive child? What purpose I wondered, could these cruel numbers serve? If I cared more about quantitative numbers I might have been crushed, but I knew better. When the social worker finished her number-filled presentation Michael and I sat quietly. Then without missing a beat she asked us to share our "dreams and visions" for Jonah's future.

"Hoping for Harvard," I was tempted to say. Instead I thought about the disconnect between the discouraging report she had just delivered and the subsequent request to wax poetic about aspirations for our boy. This only supported my sense of how clueless these trained people were about how parents of children with autism spent their time. Without much choice, we had to be completely rooted in the here and now without the luxury of musing about "dreams and visions" for Jonah's future.

Still we had been invited to go anywhere with our fantasies. Talk about Jonah's future always made us think—not necessarily about goals or achievements, but about quality of life issues. Short of a cure what we wanted for Jonah was no different than what we wanted for David and now Ruth—a sense of love, well-being, integrity and safety.

"Imagine," I told the restless group, "being dressed in your softest flannels on a blizzard night. You hear the freezing rain against the window and burrow beneath your thick comforter knowing there is no need to set the alarm for the following morning." That summed up the essence of what I wanted Jonah to have every day of his life.

They were surprised that I hadn't painted a future scenario with Jonah sharing an apartment in a semi-independent living situation with a janitorial job at some store or stadium.

But there was no quantifying what we wanted for Jonah— no list of preferences for roommates or employment assessments to figure out his work interests. What we wanted was basic, doable and could exclude people like them, who made a career of measuring people like Jonah. From that meeting on we referred to Jonah's IEPs as "Irrelevant Educational Plans." We had no illusions. The job of teaching Jonah anything worthwhile was ours alone. And with that realization, the next chapter began.

"Stop Banging the Corn" — Learning a New Vernacular

Despite the day to day chaos, I tried keeping life as normal as possible. We enjoyed family outings to the park and beach, me packing an agenda along with the sandwiches and sunscreen. Every venue became a classroom whether I was trying to teach Jonah the word "shell" on the seashore or the concept "down" on the slide. But Jonah wasn't interested. Though he smiled and laughed, it almost never had anything to do with me. I continually held things up and asked him to "look" but it was I who really needed to see. He simply was unable to take what I wanted so badly to give.

Every exchange with Jonah became a lesson, every experience a tutorial. "Aim high," I'd tell everyone who spent time with him, but Jonah was no student. He was on his own trajectory, governed by impulses beyond anyone's control.

I talked about acceptance but equated not working to improve things with giving up—something I would not do. I plied him with vitamins and diets; introduced communication boards and arranged sensory and auditory therapies. I read every miraculous recovery story and listened when the snake oil salespeople spoke, trying treatments only a hopeless thinking person would consider. Nothing, however, generated the magical forward strides I was hoping for.

The clock of what was normal in our home had to be reset. If our house was baby-proofed for Jonah's younger siblings, it was super baby-proofed for Jonah. Naturally the usual electrical and poison safeguards were in place. But there could be no hardware on cabinetry that Jonah might try to bite or break off and towel racks, which he liked to hang from, had to be adapted to support his full body weight. We added extra railing and safety features to stairs, customized window treatments because of his sensitivity to light and recessed the kitchen cook top from Jonah's wandering hands.

The absence of collected knickknacks, memorabilia and breakables was a telling reminder that autism, like the colored drawings on our refrigerator door, had a place at our house. Bare table tops, however, did not preclude warmth. As unusual as the décor may have appeared, the welcoming, safe haven feel came from the people, smells of home cooking and child paraphernalia that seemed always to be strewn about.

Being spontaneous in a household with young children is difficult—but with Jonah it was impossible. Even the simplest activities, like taking an afternoon stroll, required planning. Jonah's placid behavior could turn on a dime and whoever accompanied him had to be able to keep up with his sudden bursts of energy. "Hook Jonah up to a generator," I used to say half jokingly, "and he could illuminate a small city." There was no stopping to chitchat with neighbors – the focus always had to remain on Jonah. All it took was a turn of the head or the blink of an eye, and an unsuspecting person in Jonah's company might suddenly find themselves alone.

Even at school, where aides continuously shadowed him, and the school playground was gated, he escaped. He was found hours later on a heavy trafficked road nearby. Thankfully he was unharmed nevertheless I was upset. I was well acquainted with Jonah's Houdini-like shenanigans and feared for his future safety.

I became an emergency mama—someone who reflexively knew how to think fast on her feet. I heard the cars that raced behind me, sensed when something looked too precarious to step on and avoided anything that had the potential for causing trouble. Attempts to teach Jonah about common street hazards had little impact. We had to be his eyes and ears, always. He put small objects and dirty food wrappers in his mouth when we weren't watching and if he didn't allow us to hold his hand, we had to be sure he was in reach. All it took was one unguarded moment for him to disappear.

We took multiple walks each day, something I needed as much as him. They helped expend Jonah's excess energy, but also allowed us to spend undistracted time together. Often we'd walk in silence—other times I'd chatter about the creatures, colors and cars we saw. Jonah, however, was no audience. He preferred silence and often let me know this by taking off and running ahead.

We developed postal worker sensibilities braving sun, rain, sleet and snow, pounding the asphalt to the familiar sounds of barking dogs. On the hottest days we'd walk early to beat the heat, and on snowy afternoons, we'd layer up undaunted by the elements. Snowy days were an invitation for Jonah to roll around the frosted ground, revelry I referred to as his "primitive joy." People passing in cars sometimes stopped to offer us rides, but we'd hike on, two dark exclamation marks trudging slowly across an all white landscape. These forays created many special moments.

Jonah was especially attracted to textures and anything that appeared rough to the touch. Sewer tops were a favorite because of the rutted surface and subtle sounds that came from below. Some were jutted out of the ground, pedestal-like. I'd stand him atop the steel round and hold his arms up in "Rocky's" signature sky-reaching pose. "Jonah is king of the...," I'd say, leaving out the word "mountain" for him to fill in. Sometimes he would, other times he refused. But either way I'd end the exchange by swinging him off and around in a mother-son embrace. This was as close to normal as things got.

Finally, when Jonah was too tired to continue walking, he'd hang onto me, wanting a piggyback ride back to the house. As exhausted as I was, few things made me happier than Jonah expressing any need for me. He'd climb aboard and get his ride.

Jonah's strange behaviors were constantly changing. One week he might be spitting or playing with saliva. Another week he'd vocalize loudly and bang his chest. These perseverations, which we called *isms,* waxed and waned —yet we were always trying to understand what they meant or what need they filled for him. We tried to connect the activities to new things that had been introduced—foods, cleaning products, people. But hard as we tried, there was nothing consistent we could identify. These behaviors were not allergic reactions, rather arbitrary responses to things we could not understand. The rule of "one plus one equals two," did not apply in our lives. For us, the digit after the equal sign was constantly changing.

Jonah would sometimes express opposite emotions with identical behaviors. He'd bite his wrist, for example, when happily excited or angrily frustrated, and try to engage us. He'd seek our gaze, insistent that we pay attention while he did what was nearly intolerable for us to watch. We'd gently encourage him to stop while removing his wet, tooth-marked arm from his mouth, but it didn't register. His internal despot spoke louder than us. The more we tried to distract or redirect him, the more the biting seemed to escalate. Naturally we were upset seeing him do this but it hurt doubly knowing how hard it must have been for him to have so little control. We also were never quite sure what he was trying to say.

So much of the time he seemed out of touch and yet Jonah also possessed uncanny abilities. He craved things that were tactile—rough, prickly and sandy surfaces. I'd have to hold him back from old splintered fences, sticky pinecones and thorn bushes. He'd approach strangers to touch their beards, braces on teeth or pant zippers, without any regard for personal space. Because "inappropriate" was not a concept Jonah understood or cared about, it was our job to keep him from such embarrassments. Jonah's speed however usually outpaced our good intentions. People, for the most part, were forgiving, but there were the few who looked at us as parents unable to manage their out of control child. If only they knew.

What I found surprising was how, over time, I cared so much less about what people thought. I once asked a supermarket manager to create one candy-free cashier lane. There were many parents who didn't like having to struggle with their youngsters about not buying sweets during checkout. The proprietor said he would make the change but never followed through. When Jonah turned over the candy display while waiting for me to pay the cashier, I felt unapologetic. My request had not been unreasonable and this was a problem that could have been avoided. The manager should have accommodated us, especially as regular customers. If people made rude comments, I'd respond without getting upset the way I might have in the past. Jonah helped me develop a much thicker skin.

Being with Jonah also meant being hyperconscious around food. In parks and malls I watched for babies with bottles, snacking pedestrians, concession stands and stray food wrappers. If I saw Jonah chewing without having given him something to eat, it meant he'd helped himself to something that might or might not be edible. If Jonah saw someone eating a cookie he would think nothing of grabbing it away, mid-bite — he was that fast. If he took an apple he saw in someone's purse, I only had myself to blame—I'd allowed him to get too close.

For a child with autism, Jonah's behaviors were not extraordinary. I realized this whenever I met with other parents and compared notes. We'd talk about the latest "weirdness' of the week," sometimes recounting stories that made me felt like we were being competitive in "out-strange-ing" one other. We struggled, laughed and tried, to the extent that we could, problem solve. But what connected us most were our common worries, mostly about the future. Few of us had families that were involved day to day. The distancing, most of us realized, wasn't disinterest as much as pain and uneasiness about our situations. Family members had the luxury of opting out; parents did not.

Naturally I had my complaints but chose to be practical instead of bitter and angry. How could we ensure that Jonah's unique needs were met if we were no longer around? It's a difficult question every parent asks, but in the case of children with autism, even harder to answer. Only people who knew Jonah intimately could explain his quirks and needs—but not every child with autism had such people in their lives.

In Jonah's case his siblings were babies and other family members barely knew him. Veteran staff could step in, if they chose, but I wasn't comfortable relying on unclear possibilities. Because Jonah-specific details were critical to his care, I decided to write "Operating Instructions," 11 single-spaced pages that outlined the ins and outs of caring for Jonah. I encouraged friends in my situation to do the same.

The booklet's overview addressed Jonah's likes and dislikes, keeping him safe, the precise ways he did things and most importantly, his capabilities. "Underestimate Jonah," I cautioned, "and he would be more than happy to be served hand and foot. Push him too hard, and he will shut down." Finding a balance was key, but without the specific information outlined in the booklet, that would be impossible. I was more comfortable knowing the necessary details were spelled out, but I had no illusions.

"Operating Instructions" would probably become another pile of paper that no one would read unless, G-d forbid, they had to.

We also created a letter with specifics about priorities and how to assure that Jonah would have a good quality of life. Staying principled topped our list. Jonah did not understand the concept of a bargain, but if he did something I asked, he got the reward I promised —100 percent of the time. "Put the toy on the shelf, and you get 10 pulls on the See 'n Say." "Sit quietly and you can play with the videotape packaging." (Only a parent of a child with autism would write to the Disney and Blockbuster people requesting the empty videotape boxes or *clam shells* Jonah adored). Some thought our conscientiousness was extreme given that we were never sure what Jonah actually understood. But that was precisely the point. For someone who struggled with relationships, how could we risk not delivering something promised? Besides caring about building Jonah's trust, however, we also wanted to be role models for our other children. Seeing this from early on, David and Ruth learned the importance of honesty and integrity in how to treat people.

Maintaining Jonah's dignity was another issue that could have been easily overlooked, but one we addressed specifically in the booklet. We'd always made a point of being discrete whenever Jonah had a toileting accident. Without making a fuss, we'd attend to his needs. We also made a point of making sure that he was clean and put together before leaving the house each morning. How he looked made no difference to him, but I'd seen the weight appearance exacted in so many other situations. It may not have been politically correct to talk about the importance of appearance, but my experience had taught me that children like Jonah who looked put together were treated better and more readily accepted. My job was to provide Jonah with whatever leg up I could. I expected anyone who would care for him to do no less.

Everything I did for Jonah became a symbol of caring. I took pride in feeding him the healthiest and best—the biggest strawberries and vegetable-rich homemade soups. It didn't matter that his lunchbox looked like a poster for the four basic food groups —he wanted the junk food everyone else brought. By providing only well balanced, healthy foods I frustrated him. He would get wild whenever he saw the foods he wanted but rarely got. By the time I realized that it was okay for him to have the cookies and chips he wanted so desperately, it was too late —he'd become a habitual grabber.

Anticipating such problems was hard and Jonah was continually upping the ante. Sometimes even the seemingly small concerns became big problems. Band-Aids for example, were impossible to keep on. This became a concern when he nearly severed a finger and needed to keep the wound covered to avoid infection. Keeping his stitched hand clean and covered was a tall order. No matter how impenetrable I made the bandaging, Jonah fought back, biting, pulling, and tearing until he was free. I finally threaded two heavy tube socks together and sewed them into the shoulder seam of a thick sweatshirt. Jonah was miserable and tugged at the sleeve, looking at me pleadingly for help. Explaining that this was for his benefit did no good. He felt trapped and struggled through several versions of my creation, until his hand finally healed.

Seeing how others reacted to Jonah taught me so much about myself. I hated asking for help and never wanted to play the autism card to bypass protocol. But as Jonah got bigger and harder to manage, it became more of a necessity than an option. I wasn't looking to exploit his disability, use it as a *poor me* appeal for help, but I was caught in many situations that were tough to begin with. Was it so out of line to ask people to make exceptions to rules once in a while? According to some, it was.

While waiting in a long, slow-moving line at the airport check-in, I struggled to keep Jonah from grabbing belongings of others and vocalizing loudly. I asked the airport agent if we could move to the head of the line given Jonah's hyperactivity. We had to wait, like everyone else, she insisted. Fine I thought—I'd let Jonah do his thing. I stepped back. When he started jumping, screaming, banging and touching others security came running and showed us to the front of the line. These were little triumphs that were hard not to enjoy.

The best part of such scenarios was seeing how far I had come. Nothing was beyond asking when it came to Jonah. People could stare, become impatient, act judgmental and I'd learned not to care. I 'd become inured to glaring exchanges, rejecting the obvious opinions of others. Instead of embarrassed, I became indignant. Some say that age and maturity would have changed me anyway, but I preferred to attribute the strength building to Jonah. Thanks to him I'd become a tough cookie.

Clearly our family was unlike most. All one had to do was sit at our dinner table and hear me telling Jonah to "stop banging the corn." While the sentence seems illogical, in our family it made perfect sense. Jonah, ever the seeker of new tactile experiences, liked the sliminess created by smacking corn kernels against the palm of his hand. His excitement with the harmless albeit messy activity was so overwhelming, that he could not respond to our urgings for him to "stop."

It would have been easy to eliminate the culpable vegetable from our grocery list—but that would overlook what those words came to symbolize to our family. *"Stop banging the corn,"* became another way of saying what is weird to the rest of the world, is wont for us.

No Quick Fix

Being the first male grandchild in a family of women would have earned Jonah special status in my father's old fashioned eyes—that is if he could see clearly. But Jonah's problems got in the way. That my father adored him, as he did all his grandchildren, was without question. But it was impossible for him to separate the challenges Jonah presented from the person.

Ever the businessman, my dad sometimes allowed practicality to trump emotions. So when I told him that I was writing a book about Jonah he asked, "how much can you write about a person who doesn't say a word?" Being so concrete and a man of few words himself, my father did not see that he was more like Jonah than he realized. There was no use explaining. That autism continually made headlines in the last years of his life left him no more educated about the disability. As far as he was concerned, all he needed to know about autism began and ended with Jonah.

What Jonah lacked in words, however, we had in reams of documents. Laws required a paper trail, although the educational microscope Jonah was under revealed the same basic information year after year. Many trees were sacrificed for school reports that documented routine activities, dressing and eating independently, brushing teeth, putting on shoes, etc. Page after page was filled with little relevant content, bureaucratic jargon and numbers that sometimes meant nothing to us. Often we felt like outsiders—as if school professionals colluded in a conspiracy of exclusion. The less we understood, the more sophisticated the school system appeared. But Jonah's deficits were obvious and the last thing we needed was quantitative mumbo jumbo to explain things. Besides, all we really wanted to know was how to best help him. The administrative signatures may have made the paperwork official, important, worth saving. But unlike most parents who collected report cards, trophies, school play videos, I had paper—without a single line drawn by Jonah.

As Jonah's developmental gap continually widened we were reminded of autism's ability to turn even nature's power, on its ear. Typically a child grows more independent with age allowing the parents to take a less active roll. But with Jonah, the opposite happened. His needs and activity level ramped up while we felt more and more depleted. Jonah's awareness of his physical autonomy became more pronounced and he began to assert himself in a way I had never had to deal with before. He was bigger and stronger, and knew it.

We also saw dramatic changes in his sleep habits. He'd followed the normal sleep patterns of developing children until he turned 10. Perhaps his adolescent hormones were starting to kick in, but sleeping reliably through the night became a thing of the past. He would stay up sometimes for several nights in a row. It would have been fine if he could stay quietly in his room, but when he was up, one of us had to be on "Jonah watch." Besides keeping him safe we had to limit the noise he made from waking the other children. Playing videotapes might have helped, but we were afraid that might give him a reason to get up and reinforce his wakefulness. Telling him "it was night, we were tired, let others sleep," meant absolutely nothing to him. As far as he was concerned, day had become a 24-hour proposition.

Jonah's neurologist explained that insomnia in people with autism was common and difficult to manage. Medication was an option but it might take a long time until we found the right mix. We rejected the idea, having demonized drugs as being artificial, unpredictable and without guarantees. We clung to our old mantra—"medication is bad; natural is good"—and were strengthened in our convictions after reading the potential side effects of existing sleep aids.

Instead we took the natural approach, trying to physically exhaust him with swimming and several long walks each day. The effects of all this effort, however, were hard to measure. Some nights he slept, just as he did before, but other times he seemed overtired, almost too stimulated to settle down.

We hired night help although it seemed that Jonah reserved his insomnia for those nights we were on our own. Scheduling people to stay the night required advanced notice but there was no way of anticipating which times we would actually need the help. It didn't take long to see that the arrangement was a losing proposition— most of the time we ended up paying for something we didn't need.

A friend said she'd seen such insomnia in children who developed food allergies. We experimented by removing all wheat and dairy from Jonah's diet, though milk, cereal, bread and cheese were his favorite foods. A month later Jonah was miserable in addition to being sleepless.

We tried dosing him with vitamins and a nutritional concoction that tasted as vile as it smelled. I tried hiding the crushed horse pills in ice cream sandwiches, but even trusting Jonah, who ate just about anything I gave him, clamped his mouth shut. I would have done the same. In the meantime our list of possible causes and solutions for his sleeplessness became shorter and shorter.

Running on empty made all of us irritable, especially me. I was living proof that "when momma ain't happy, ain't nobody happy." Exhaustion skews one's thinking and I was probably worse than most. Sometimes I'd get angry with Jonah for disrupting the peaceful few hours I had come to rely on. Each night I'd want him gone, anywhere out of earshot. I started thinking about Higashi but just the thought of sending him away frightened me. I genuinely wished I could help Jonah, but I also wanted to protect all of our sleep and sanity.

I rarely spoke about my feelings to others, but when I did no one was allowed to say a word. If someone suggested sending him away to school, I'd see myself as a tigress mama. I had similar reactions as a teenager, when only I was allowed to criticize members of my family. I could say anything I wanted, but I'd stop talking to anyone who agreed with me or added negative comments about someone I cared about. Though the situation with Jonah was different, the dynamics were similar. I didn't want input—I just wanted to be heard.

To get some relief, someone suggested that we look into a shared parenting program offered through one of the local special needs agencies. Strangers as secondary parents, however, conjured images of foster abuses. Still, Mike and I agreed we had more than ourselves to consider. David and Ruth were too little to complain, but they really needed some exclusive time and focus. What I wished for but didn't have was an indulgent grandmother or doting aunt to take Jonah away for a few nights at a time once in a while.

David and Ruth were enrolled in a religious preschool program and though we did our best to observe Sabbath traditionally by lighting candles, eating Friday night meals together at a beautifully set table and going to synagogue, the sound of videotapes and people coming and going in their cars caused noisy distractions. The hubbub ran counterpoint to the restful Sabbath atmosphere we tried to create.

We asked friends if they knew anyone who might be interested in hosting Jonah one weekend a month. Someone my husband worked with said she was. A devout Christian and energetic mother of teen girls, she visited us with her family and took immediately to Jonah. She enjoyed doing ministry work and genuinely wanted to help out. But as eager as I was to start such an arrangement, I wanted her to think about what she was taking on and discuss it with her family. Too many bad decisions had been made in haste, and this was a considerable commitment that would eat away at her free time, which was already very limited.

A few days later she called and said she was sure about her decision to have Jonah spend time with her family each month. We were touched and delighted. We understood that there would be an initial trial period and that she might decide that caring for Jonah was too much. But our worries were without basis —her family was happy having Jonah from the start. Their offer was a godsend. Once a month for the next two years they picked Jonah up before we left for synagogue on Saturday and we went to pick him up for dinner with us the following day.

Jonah not only became a member of their extended family, but was welcomed by their community as well. I was grateful knowing Jonah could "belong" somewhere other than our home. The family looked forward to having him, and we got much needed, albeit short, breaks.

At around this same time the autism community was abuzz with the newest autism breakthrough —facilitated communication (FC). By typing on a keyboard, non-verbal individuals such as those with autism, were said to communicate. Proponents talked about finally getting a glimpse into the sometimes-sophisticated minds of individuals with autism. Though I always believed Jonah had complex thoughts he was not able to express, I wasn't as interested in profundities as I was in getting "yes" or "no" answers to simple questions. Though the claims of success I'd been hearing seemed extreme, nothing would have made me happier than to actually find something that delivered on its promises.

People from the Facilitated Communication Institute at University of Syracuse were visiting and offered to run trials with the students in Jonah's school program. They began by giving a brief overview of FC and reporting impressive statistics about its efficacy in accessing otherwise non-communicative people. Though I am not a scientist, the success rate claims seemed extreme.

Nevertheless, as long as it was non—invasive and would do no harm, I was willing to give it a try.

I observed through a one—way mirror. Jonah was unhappy and uncomfortable when he was seated at the keyboard with the trained facilitator. He began twisting away, his body slowly inching under the table while he aggressively bit his one free hand. I naturally wanted to jump in and help out.

In a soft, non-threatening voice the facilitator, asked him, "how many nickels are there in a dime." She appeared to be supporting his arm, passively, giving him free rein to do whatever he wanted in response to the questions asked. Jonah was partially under the table and couldn't see the keyboard though the facilitator still supported the outstretched finger on his hand.

I heard the slow tapping on the keyboard. With her bolstering his hand he typed "tu." Phonetic misspellings, I was told were common. "What color is the sky?" she asked. Once again, with facilitator's support, he tapped out "bloo."

I'd had enough. Though Jonah might have known more than he let on, he had no exposure to money and was unable to identify colors. Anyone who really knew Jonah agreed there was no way he could have answered either of those questions. The facilitator insisted that I was out of touch with how much Jonah understood. I wished she were right.

My tone was angry as I asked how Jonah managed to type without having before seen, much less touched a keyboard. She didn't answer my question, rather claimed I was underestimating him. I sensed that she was playing the guilt card, which was easy with someone like me. I suggested that she ask him the name of one of his caregivers. There had been so many people who had come and gone over the years that almost any name, Sue, Amy, Tina, would have been correct. But she said she wasn't comfortable asking that question because of the undue pressure it might create. I knew my kid and what he could and could not do. I didn't feel my request was all that unreasonable. I passed when it came to signing up for the weekend workshop they were offering.

I watched as other hopeful parents observed their children. Many of them were friends and did sign up for private training. I had a policy of not sharing my opinions. I felt that people had to do what they believed was best for their child. Each situation was different. In our case I believed that I saved the cost of a keyboard, hours of supervision not to mention having to struggle with Jonah. But just because I did not think FC was right for our situation, I had no problem with those who chose to pursue it. Historically scientific breakthroughs were radical departures from conventional wisdom. I would have been delighted if FC turned out to work for anyone.

After our brief trial with FC, I read Annabel Stehli's "The Sound of a Miracle: A Child's Triumph Over Autism," which attributes one child's cure to auditory training. Some friends had taken their children to Canada for two weeks to have the treatment and swore by its benefits. With two small children to care for at home, that was not doable for me. But when I heard that a local audiologist had been trained and was doing auditory training in our area, I thought it was something worth considering.

This new treatment supposedly helped enhance the focusing abilities of children with autism. The therapy, developed by Guy Berard, presumes that people with learning problems have "abnormal" or "asymmetrical" hearing. The goal is to normalize the hearing by mobilizing and exercising the inner ear and brain with customized sounds and frequencies. This is done using headphones.

After an evaluation and audiogram, Jonah's 20-session treatment was set up. He had to stay home from school for the two weeks of treatment. At the office he wore headphones for a half-hour in the morning and half-hour in the afternoon. Weekends were off. Keeping Jonah home for two weeks, in itself, was a major trial. But the struggle to keep the headphones on his head was worse. Each half hour became more of an upsetting wrestling match than a relaxed, "listening to sounds" session.

Once the sound series was completed, the therapist explained that it might take up to a year for us to see changes. The treatment, he explained, could be credited with any positive changes we might see. But we were also told that an increase in negative behaviors meant the therapy was beginning to kick in. According to that logic, any behaviors, good or bad, were attributable to the therapy working. It was easy to see why one could become cynical.

Parents I knew actually went for second and third rounds of this treatment, believing in its merit. I however felt Jonah might have derived greater benefit if I had used the one thousand single dollar bills the treatment cost to light a fire. At least we would have gotten some warmth from its glow.

Besides the small fortune it cost us, this continuous quest for a solution felt like an emotional roller coaster ride—hopeful at the outset, jaded by the end. All the treatment chasing however became instructive. If we are conditioned from early on to believe that headache relief should be just a pill and swallow away, why is it unreasonable to extrapolate that there should be one-pill like solutions to other problems as well? Until the day she died, my mother was convinced that there would be a single dose injection that would reverse autism. Thus far autism has eluded such simple solutions.

Though it has been almost seven decades since Leo Kanner first described autism, there still are no scientific treatments that consistently benefit individuals with this disability. We, like most parents of children with autism, are still waiting.

Despite the onslaught of interventions, Jonah's sleep problems persisted. We'd avoided the question for months but finally asked ourselves how desperate we would have to become to take the medication plunge?

The chloral hydrate we picked up at the drugstore was in a brown bottle reminiscent of old cartoon cures marked XXX. This, however, was serious business. We were tentative as we fed him the first of many spoonfuls. What were we giving him and what would his reaction be? There would be no way to know unless we tried. We had no idea at the time that giving him the medication would be the tip on the iceberg of things we once swore we would never try.

Mother or Martyr?

My mom was the quintessential self-sacrificing Jewish mother, a person who put everyone before herself. English was her second language and when I'd tell her, "Don't be such a martyr," she'd mishear me and respond by saying, "wait until you're a mother." She confused the word "martyr" with "mother," unwittingly presaging a connection that would surface once again in later years.

Martyrdom wears various hats— and the one I chose to wear was as the parent to a son with autism. With Jonah in my life I became the lead in my mother's script—lacking sleep, being dependent on help, living without privacy— the list goes on. I, however, was not all that unique.

I belonged to a community of parents with disabled children who spoke and understood the language of sacrifice. Most of us agreed that we would not have volunteered for what we were handed and struggled, each in our own way, to make things work. Though we had different backgrounds, educations and means, we understood the guilt of wishing things were different. We sometimes talked about people who adopted multiple special needs children and, how they, according to magazine and television feature articles, managed so well.

"They don't make the same emotional investment as birth parents." "Their children are easier." "They have better support systems," were some of the unsubstantiated rationales. The important question we neglected to ask was why this mattered. Why did some of us view others' triumphs as our failures? There was no one size fits all answer—yet it was clear that we all struggled with issues of self-confidence and competence. One thing I knew for sure. Though I admired her, I was no Mia Farrow.

The only life I really knew was my own and yet I, like many of these friends, credited strangers in articles and on television magazines with being so much better at handling life's stresses. Did having a disabled child cloud my objectivity?

Even visits to the pediatrician's office became grist for my self-deprecatory mill. In the waiting room, competitive mothers staged "read alongs" with their precocious toddlers in voices they made sure others would hear. Some arrived with adult entourages, others in top-grade strollers. People were friendly and niceties were exchanged but there was also an undercurrent of undeclared pressure to be "model mom." I'd sit next to Jonah with his fidgets and noises smiling sheepishly, doing whatever I could to keep him from bothering others. But my uneasiness had nothing to do with Jonah. Not measuring up was my issue and while therapy would continue to help me, so was having a self-assured role model as a friend.

Rachel, a mother of 12, ran a chaotic yet welcoming household. Some saw her as "superwoman" measuring her success in the extraordinary number of children she was raising so well. But that was only part of the story. From early on she knew what she wanted and had the confidence to follow through. She was a realist who openly admitted that she wasn't after perfection. She worked hard, did the best she could but it wasn't unusual to find her children eating a January breakfast of popsicles or her second grader managing several younger siblings. Some may have considered this negligent, but Rachel and her husband were wonderful parents; consistent, patient, loving and it showed.

As far as she was concerned she had no appearances to keep up, no pedestals from which to fall or yardsticks by which to be measured. She didn't sweat the small stuff and the big stuff she saw as God-driven. Her easy, "nothing to prove" manner was inspiring and I saw how life carried on even without all the T's crossed or I's dotted. Using her as a role model and inspiration, I tried to adopt her "do the best you can" credo and made "good enough" my new standard. This was what people meant when they said maturity comes with age.

Still, I was left with having to balance difficult choices for Jonah and our family. Giving him sleep medication, for example, had a down side— dizziness and lethargy. What if the solution ended up being worse than the problem? Was I selfishly putting our need to sleep before Jonah's natural inclination not to? And what message was I sending to my other children about tolerance and micromanaging behavior? I wanted straightforward black and white answers, when most, I was quickly learning, tended to be gray. Second-guessing was what parents did, and good luck had as much to do with getting it right as good sense.

Whether to take or leave Jonah behind for family vacations was another difficult question that kept coming up over and over again. When he traveled with us everything had to revolve around him, yet when we left him home the guilt and worry exacted a different price. "Out of sight, out of mind" was a dictum that simply did not apply to us. And unexpected problems, we knew from past experience, were more probable than possible.

During one of our first getaways without Jonah the sitter called to say "he didn't seem quite right." The doctor who knew him fairly well found nothing wrong, yet we ignored her "let's wait and see" advice and boarded the next flight home. It was a good thing.

Diagnosing ailments in Jonah is difficult under the best circumstances, but with waxing and waning pain it becomes an even harder guessing game. When we arrived Jonah was hunched over and alarmingly quiet. I was beyond seeing the logic of "the same thing could have happened if we had been home." "I could have," "I should have," became the kicks I'd grown accustomed to giving myself. By the next morning his appendix was removed.

Sitting beside him in the hospital, waiting for him to rouse from surgery, I couldn't help but wonder what it would be like if the anesthesia blocked some enzyme or reversed some metabolic quirk that caused his autism. I imagined what it would be like if when he woke, he'd sit up and say, "Hi Mom. What's happening?" He might look me in the eyes, something he rarely did, and like magic, our years of worry and heartache would be over.

I kissed him and like a storybook prince, he opened his eyes. The spell ended there. Jonah was back, autism and all.

Creating family time was another challenge. We were good at hanging around the house, being together, not necessarily engaged in the same things. On occasion we'd venture out, but the desire to linger at the zoo's monkey cage or museums' hands-on display was impossible when Jonah wanted to move on. And while I wished we could eat together as a family, dinner for Jonah was an all business, eat and run affair. The picture I had in my head of family time never jibed with what actually happened.

Sending him off with caregivers was not what was suggested in "good parenting" guides, but I tried to stop being so self-critical. There was nothing typical about our family and though it was very difficult, I began to get comfortable with the concept of not being cookie cutter perfect.

The one activity, however, we did enjoy sharing was swimming. We'd started taking Jonah to the pool early on and the doctor expressed concern about his severe gross motor delays. Walking would have helped but he was one and a half and still crawling. Water activity was a good alternative.

From the start Jonah, like the whale from the eponymous biblical story, was a natural. He enjoyed the water but refused any attempt to be taught. I purchased a vest circled with small vertical Styrofoam logs. Slowly, over time, I removed them allowing him to adapt to the small reductions in support. By the time all the inserts were removed, he could remain buoyant and glide, swan like, from one end of the pool to the other. Few things gave me greater pleasure than watching his body move fluidly against the aqua colored background. We became regulars at the community center, showing up with our swim gear even on the coldest winter days. That Jonah loved swimming was a godsend; besides allowing us to share fun times in the water, he expended excess energy and developed much improved gross motor skills.

The one problem we had was accessing the pool, which required walking through either the men or ladies' locker room. Most of Jonah's caregivers were women but Jonah could not walk through the men's locker room alone. In general we changed him in the women's locker room but as he got older and bigger I worried about making others uncomfortable. I'd ready him, (and his siblings when they came along); at home and quickly undress them in a far corner of the locker room when we got to the pool.

For many years no one said a word. But when Jonah was almost 10 an old woman, we'd never seen before, went into a red-faced rage about his being there. She called me "irresponsible" and "inappropriate" and threatened to tell the people in charge. I acknowledged her upset and tried to explain the situation, but she wasn't interested. If only Jonah noticed naked women I thought to myself. The woman continued her rant until David, usually a quiet observer, stood with his hands on his hips and told her, "Leave my big brother alone." I beamed. My three-year old was already becoming Jonah's advocate.

There was no doubt that the need for a family changing room existed, not just for people like Jonah, but for single parents wanting to swim with their opposite sexed children. I met with the community center director but there were no funds. I asked him to keep the idea in mind and he did. Two years later, when the building underwent major renovations, three family changing rooms were added. Though it was never officially stated, the locker room drama ignited a small and necessary spark. Jonah indirectly had an important and positive impact.

Just as Jonah's age played a role in the locker room confrontation it also influenced our ability to recruit help. His toddler charm had been replaced by his grade school size and the demands of caring for him had changed as well. Some people had issues about a boy his size having toileting accidents. I understood. Cleaning up a mess on a strong resistive ten-year old was a lot to ask. Add to that the public embarrassment of having the pool "shut down" because of a bathroom mishap. This sometimes became more than caregivers could take. Only people made of tough stuff could really handle the ride.

Consequently I became increasingly dependent on the very short list of people we had to help out. Michael and I argued about the best way to handle Jonah. While I played indulgent mother, he felt we should continue to challenge him. He would offer Jonah a treat but expect him to first say some word in exchange. I would cringe watching Jonah stammering, barely able to utter a syllable, let alone a word. Michael was frustrated by my lack of support—I was aggravated by his inflexibility.

We were both well intentioned, motivated by our love and what we believed was best for Jonah, but at times it was tough going. Parental consistency was important but so was respecting each other's views. We were continually searching for what was best for Jonah trying not to step on each other's toes.

Besides being sleep deprived and short on help we had to be honest about Jonah's lack of progress and sadly, regression. The little language he had was diminished and spontaneous speech, though rare in the past, was all but gone. His toileting accidents varied in frequency, and he began ruminating—bringing food he swallowed back up into his mouth. We were accustomed to the coming and going of bizarre behaviors, but instead of waning, this particular problem escalated. A behavioral expert that was brought in by the school district described the regurgitation as "the behavior of all behaviors." Jonah had everyone, including school staffers, worried.

Besides causing an off-putting odor, the ruminating could create a serious health problem. We brought Jonah to a gastroenterologist who said that chronic gastric acids in his throat could, over time, cause esophageal cancer. The school called in the behavioral big guns – "experts" who scheduled numerous consultations. We spent hours and hours brainstorming, trying to figure out strategic ways to help Jonah. There were no simple answers.

To deter the regurgitating, one suggested spraying him with cold water; another putting drops of Tabasco on his tongue after we noticed his cheeks ballooning with vomit. We couldn't believe what we were hearing. What others called "ingenious," we called punitive and "insane."

There was no way we would allow such measures to be taken.

Jonah's only "mainstreaming" was riding the regular education bus to and from school.   "I like your son so much," the student helper assigned to Jonah told me as I escorted my son off the bus. "But," the boy continued, "you shouldn't give him Greek salad for lunch every day." The feta the boy thought he smelled was actually the sour breath caused by Jonah's continuous ruminating.

There was no simple solution and much to consider. This behavior, like so many before, would demand increased vigilance and redirection.   How much more could we do and at what cost to our other children? Perhaps he needed more than we were able to give.

The thought was devastating, but was it time to revisit Higashi? I reread the materials and notes I'd collected four years earlier. Martyr or mother, which would I be? We were about to make the hardest decision of our lives.

Bittersweet

With mounting daily stresses and strains, I was forced to reconsider our firmly held belief that we would never treat Jonah differently than our other two children. But that overlooked how off balance our family scale had become. We still believed everything was worth trying but were growing tired and disheartened by the lack of results. With "other children to think about," our parents encouraged us to reconsider Higashi. It was practical advice we'd heard many times before, but were never emotionally ready to put into play. Things, however, could not continue as they were. Even in the book of "Genesis," Abraham's beloved son Ishmael is sent away to protect his other son Isaac. I was afraid another visit to Higashi would put us one step closer to signing on some dotted line. Saying I was terrified didn't begin to describe the emotions unleashed by this consideration.

What had become of single-minded, advocate me—the person who refused to take "no" for an answer ; was unwilling to compromise in all matters related to Jonah? Was I really ready to allow complete strangers to care for my non-communicative son? Even if sending him away to school made sense to us, how would we explain our decision to his brother and sister? How would those who admired our devotion for so long understand such a dramatic turnaround?

I rationalized by saying children were sent to boarding schools and colleges all the time, but I knew how hollow that comparison was. Relinquishing all control of Jonah's day-to-day care was comparable to my giving up—at least that is what I believed on some level. I was a cruel judge, mainly to myself, and could only guess what others would think. I could make up excuses, say Jonah needed more than we could give, that he would be better off with round the clock care and education. But that overlooked the selfish component of the equation. Things had become untenable at home.

I made arrangements for the visit to Boston, too upset and embarrassed to tell anyone other than our parents. The day we left for the visit, I sat in the airport and saw things I never took note of before. I watched travelers as they negotiated the terminal rush and chaos easily locating their gates, plane seats and luggage. Jonah was also a traveler; only he lacked what all those people probably took for granted— the basic know-how necessary to navigate from point A to B. How frightening the constant transitions of daily living must have been for him, having to rely on another person always, never knowing where to go or what the next moment would bring. It had become my habit, to identify with Jonah, to try experiencing the world as I imagined he did. Make me an alien on another planet, I decided, and I might begin to understand.

Higashi's reputation had grown in the four years since we first visited the school and in that time enrollment had increased and a credentialed board had formed. None of this, however, impressed us. All we really cared about was what the school could offer Jonah. We arrived as business people, allowing ourselves to be pitched to with meetings, classroom visitations and dormitory tours. But there was no disguising how personally this was being felt. I could not let go of Jonah easily.

The physical set up was as I remembered it, bright, cheery with hand-drawn pictures, student projects and photographs lining the hallways. The teachers in gym clothing conveyed a warm, yet assertive, "stay on top of it" vigilance. The place had more of a camp than school feel with spirited cheers helping to coax the short lines of uniformed students from class to class, activity to activity. They were clean, well groomed but more importantly, seemed relaxed around staff. There was no pretending with this group; what you saw from the students was as straight from the gut as it came. When one of youngsters had an outburst, I was relieved as I watched unflappable staff members calm him. We may have been seeing things on a good day, but I still found that unscripted exchange reassuring.

Though it might have seemed a petty detail, I cared about what kind of food the school served. Few things pleased Jonah more than what he ate, and I could not fathom having one of his greatest pleasures compromised. We were invited to sit with the students and staff for lunch and were happily surprised by what we saw. Rather than the expected institutional fare, there was home cooking, the hired cook a grandmother to one of the Higashi students. Besides being healthy and plentiful, the food looked and smelled appealing. After a two-day survey of meals and snacks, I was happy to have one less item on my checklist of things to worry about.

What I found remarkable about mealtime was watching the students' self control— sitting with food-filled plates in front of them without grabbing. They had been trained to sit with their hands clasped above the table until staff signaled them with a school-like cheer to begin eating. None of the students seemed upset or agitated by the restrictive routine. I questioned whether Jonah could ever show such self-restraint—it had never been expected of him. As a student of Option™ he had lived an "anything goes" lifestyle, nothing like the school's prescribed rules and regulations.

Higashi's program was about structure, focus, giving the child tools to help manage impulses. If things got out of control the students were asked to "pose," or stand in positions that demanded mindfulness and balance. The idea was to distract them from difficult behaviors. We saw a few "incidents" and accompanying tantrums, but were assured that posing was far better than using medication to manage behavior. We were happy about the school's strict "no drugs for behavior" policy. Medication was given exclusively for illness or chronic medical conditions.

Physical activity played a major role in the school curriculum. It was the natural, common sense approach to dissipating the anxiety and hyperactivity often seen among the students. I knew firsthand how beneficial a good workout could be. Teach the children parameters, give them tools and the child with autism will grow, Kito Kitahara, the school founder, believed. But once again, formulas are easy to establish yet hard to implement, especially when someone is as stubborn and resistive as Jonah. When he didn't want to do something he would drop to the ground and refuse to budge.

Higashi's administrators were encouraging. They told us they were confident Jonah could benefit from what they had to offer and even be toilet trained. This was hard to believe. We'd devoted ourselves full-time to cultivating this skill and despite some progress, he still had a long way to go. Becoming independent in this area alone would make sending him to the school worthwhile.

We'd spent an intensive two days getting familiar with the school routine and staff but we weren't yet convinced that Higashi would be the way to go. Just before heading home we witnessed an exchange that told us what we really wanted to know. A student who had been touching himself inappropriately broke away from his line to shake the hand of the school director who was passing. I waited to see how this Brooks Brothers-clad administrator would respond. I searched his face for a sign, that subtle yet telling wince that would give me the only reason I needed to forget about the place. But without the slightest hint of discomfort, he shook the boy's hand and returned him to his group. It was hard not to be impressed. The administrator did not realize that he had just passed an important test.

Part of me wished I could fall in love with the school——it would have made deciding whether or not to send Jonah so much easier. But I was cautious, having fallen too easily many times before. When the overly gung ho speech therapist suddenly lost interest or when the devoted home-helper disappeared without notice, I was always more than hurt or disappointed. I felt betrayed. Besides, how could I hang my hopes on a place I also saw as taking my child away, conveniently ignoring that it was our choice whether or not to send him.

With our due diligence nearly complete, we called a few Higashi parents, including one couple who, like us, had done the Option™ program with their child. They were on the same "leave no stone unturned" path and Higashi was another notch on their "tried everything humanly possible" belt. Most parents talked about the school as a "godsend" with the positives far outweighing the negatives. Still the most difficult question remained, "Should we send him?" This would become the toughest decision of our married lives.

We drew a black vertical line between our list of pros and cons. I wanted Jonah to stay; I wanted him to go. I wanted to supervise him, yet wanted him to have a better chance at "education." I wanted to be in control but wanted to be free. I knew the care, no matter how good, would never equal what he got at home but we had come to a crossroads. No matter what I did, it would never be enough. The days of things being clear-cut were long over; difficult decisions had become a fundamental part of our lives. The only thing I knew for sure was there was no right or wrong. Higashi would not be a solution; at best it would be a compromise. There would be painful trade-offs and the saddest part was that Jonah would not even have a say.

We'd give it a try, send Jonah for a trial period and then decide. Because the school was year round and had a rolling admissions policy we could start Jonah anytime. He would go in May, and all of us would have a chance to test the waters until the second week of August when he would return home for the five-week summer break. (The school was considered "year round" though in some "months," classes were in session for a week or two.) Though the "trial run" meant we could opt out, I sensed this arrangement would be more than temporary. Though I had the final say, I felt resigned, like a woman in a poorly arranged marriage. Instead of looking forward to the walk down the aisle, I approached the "groom" terrified and dreading having to say, "I do."

I worried about what would run through Jonah's head the first morning he woke in a strange bed, in a new place with unfamiliar people. I couldn't begin to guess. We'd turn his world upside down. If only I could explain things to him; if only he understood.

This was a decision that was supposed to be for his benefit and yet there was no denying that as soon as he left for Boston, our lives improved. In his absence we saw how consumed we had been with his education and care. We were grateful to be able to sit quietly, without interruptions or people coming and going. Night after night we slept undisturbed in our own beds. We left the house for hours, without checking our watches or feeling guilty. The chronic dread of mishandling something or someone connected with Jonah was, at least temporarily, gone. We took none of this for granted. It was the first time in years that the chronic heaviness on my chest lifted. I could breathe, deep cleansing breaths, and I loved the feeling.

We called the school regularly and had no choice but to believe reports that he was adjusting well. I was sorry I had not stayed in touch with Boston friends from my graduate school days. I might have had objective eyes to check in on Jonah on our behalf. Instead I had to rely on the word of school staff, many of whom I'd never met.

Jonah sometimes allowed the phone to be placed by his ear. Who would have guessed that listening to someone's breathing would become the "conversation" I most looked forward to? Other times he would throw the phone to the ground. In my mind he had reason to reject a phone with me on the other end. There was no way however, to know what Jonah was thinking or feeling. He was whatever I imagined him to be at that moment.

When he returned for summer break, he was his old self, still not toilet trained or sleeping through the night. He had been gone for two months yet were able to snap back into "high Jonah alert" mode immediately. The transition felt like getting on a bicycle after a few years of not riding. For us, caring for Jonah was difficult but second nature. We were lucky that some of Jonah's helpers were around for the summer and willing to work.

We knew we missed him terribly when he was away yet enjoyed the simple pleasures of a "normal" life. We wanted him to stay at home but the local school had nothing to offer. He was the student that didn't fit anywhere; the district's poster boy for the "exception to the exceptional." For so many reasons, sending him to Higashi for the year made sense.

Such seismic decisions are often accompanied by aftershocks which for us meant thinking about moving to Boston. On so many levels it made sense; we would be close to Jonah as well as our families in New York. The exorbitant tuition would be covered entirely if we became Massachusetts residents. Many Higashi families relocated or divided the family so that one guardian established Massachusetts residency while the other parent traveled back and forth on weekends. We knew that wasn't for us.

Leaving Michigan at that point would be hard. Mike loved his work and was involved in a variety of projects. My work was portable but close friends, many of whom were like family, would be a major loss for me. Tuition would be an issue, but we would appeal to the local school district for help. Michael interviewed for a couple of jobs but the more we talked about moving, the more we realized we wanted to stay put. Besides, what sense did it make to start all over again when Higashi students aged out of the school at 21. We were dizzy with all there was to think about.

I distracted myself by shopping for the long list of things Jonah would need for school, but that was the easy part. Writing his name over and over again on his whale-themed belongings made me feel like I was signing his life away. The decision had been made without his vote. His belongings were organized into neat little piles that were ready to be packed. Even his soap-dish read Jonah Moshe Lehmann, the name he couldn't even say unless it was modeled.

I'd always told people that Jonah understood more than he let on. Now that he was going away I wanted to believe that our not being there day-to-day, wouldn't matter much to him. With the Higashi decision I became a bundle of contradictions.

Summer ended and my sister and I accompanied Jonah to Boston. We would stay a few days to help transition him, or so we thought. School staff felt we would confuse and distract him so we stayed out of the way, but close by. During one of his classes I peered into the small glass window of the room and saw that the person assigned to Jonah's group was primarily focused on him. The teacher already understood how closely Jonah needed to be watched.

On our way to the airport home, my sister and I stopped by a drug store. A group of menacing looking teens, not much older than Jonah, sat on the ground by the entrance. They were, smoking and given the late morning hour, probably skipping classes. But instead of fearing them, as I might have in the past, I became angry. They chose to blow opportunities I would have given anything for Jonah to have. I'd felt that way a million times before. I walked into the store and spared them the lecture.

I flew back to Detroit and settled into a routine that had the framework but not the details of life with Jonah. There were no schedules to organize or cars lined up in our driveway. I could lock the doors and when the bell rang, nine times out of 10 it was an invited guest or mail delivery. I enjoyed the quiet, thoroughly. Sometimes I'd go into Jonah's room my head spinning with Hallmark sentiments.

I thought about the sweet and tender moments Jonah and I shared, choosing to ignore the anguish and frustration he'd elicited countless times. Clearly I preferred it that way; connecting only good thoughts with my faraway son.

Letting Go

Jonah may have been gone but he was everywhere. Every neighborhood walk I took was accompanied by thoughts of him. There was the long rocky ditch Jonah loved walking on and the house he ran to, remembering he'd once been given candy there. I thought about him when I filled my grocery basket without his favorite foods and ordered fewer tickets for our regular outing to "Sesame Street Live." I took David and Ruth to playgrounds Jonah had never been to and reserved zoo and petting farm visits for his vacations home.

I appreciated when people asked how he was doing but if they didn't, I'd mention him anyway. Instead, of holding his hand or kissing his cheek I used talk to ensure that he wasn't overlooked or forgotten. Saying his name fed the illusion that our connection remained strong.

I'd see boys his age and imagine him in their clothes, with their mannerisms. I'd think about what it would be like to stroll the aisles of a library looking for books on science or sports or convince him to eat something other than burgers and fries. While asleep I'd dream him into a talking dynamo, who instead of wearing Kmart shirts tucked into elastic waist sweat pants with Velcro closure sneakers was dressed for a Ralph Lauren print ad. I'd refer to him as "dreamboat" and feel an unfamiliar happiness, as if I could lasso some new galaxy of stars.

With Jonah away, I had a recurring nightmare about him standing on a steeply angled roof in the pouring rain. I know calling him from below is no solution; he'll either ignore me or turn without watching his step. Running to the roof to rescue him means losing sight of him for just a few seconds—but that is too long for him to be unattended. While I weigh what to do, he steps forward and without expression, falls to the ground. Though I am asleep my knees go weak and I hear myself scream "don't move." I am thinking about spinal injuries when he sits up precipitously, oblivious to what has just happened. I'd wake up breathless, sweaty and sick that Jonah may have unwittingly turned an already bad situation into something much worse. I am unable to rescue my child in my dreams, just as I have never been able to in full consciousness.

Thinking about him, however, was not enough. I couldn't wait until Christmas, Easter and summer breaks to see him so we flew to Boston for "in between vacation" visits. Each semester I wanted to spend time on his turf, lie on his bed, see what he saw when he opened his eyes in the morning and sample his experiences first hand. We tested the school's open door policy and got to know a couple of local parents who agreed to check on Jonah on our behalf.

We stayed in a nearby hotel with an indoor pool, ate, swam, and when weather allowed, played in the park or by the river. I'd bring his favorite books and tapes, cut his hair and nails and let him play in the tub for as long as he wanted. By the time we brought him back to the dorm he looked fresh scrubbed and groomed, or as the dorm counselor put it, "good as new."

The goodbyes, however, were impossibly sad. When he was relaxed and easy to handle I felt we should pack him up, bring him home and start over. When he was agitated and uncooperative, I was sad again, this time because he hadn't made more progress. Higashi wasn't what we wanted, but there were really no better alternatives. Take him home and then what? We'd fly back to Detroit feeling heavy hearted and compromised, hungry for David and Ruth's spontaneous embraces. We tried to focus on what we had to be thankful for.

Jonah's vacations home, especially the first few times, were a mix of excitement and anxiety. I'd want to fill the weeks he was home with everything he might have missed during his time away. I would cook his favorite foods and take him to our old neighborhood haunts for people to see how great he looked and how much he had grown. Finding help, however, was a problem. Most of Jonah's caregivers were working elsewhere. We threw our nets wide with poor results. Recruiting help for a 12-year old who still had periodic toileting accidents made it so much harder than when he was three. Hiring strangers was pointless. Getting to know Jonah took time and by the time they understood his needs and rhythms, Jonah would be returning to school. Higashi discouraged hiring their staff during breaks but knew how demanding Jonah could be. After several difficult vacations, Higashi allowed us to hire someone who knew Jonah well. The aide was grateful for the extra work but, still, could not care for Jonah for all the hours we needed. When he was home our help situation was skeletal at best.

The fantasy of how things should be during these visits never jibed with what actually occurred. Most of the time we just got by. Days were long. If Jonah slept through the night we considered ourselves lucky. But that still left 16 hours in the day to fill, quite a challenge for a boy without friends, interests or designated places to be. We went swimming, walking, for car rides, to get ice cream, outdoor concerts and malls. But much of our time was spent in front of the television watching every Disney video imaginable. By the time Jonah went back to school I knew the Disney compendium, chapter and verse. When I filled in the forms for school about what Jonah had done on vacation, I made it sound fun and cozy. But nothing held Jonah's interest for long. Most of the time he'd pull me, saying, "Want to go," one of his very few spontaneous spoken phrases. "But where?" was the question no one including him, could answer.

His siblings didn't really understand what "Jonah is coming home" meant and had a hard time accepting that the changes in our household would be short term. Before he arrived I'd tell them I might be not be as available as usual. Better, I thought, for them to expect less and have me more, but things backfired. They became more demanding while I became, of all things, painfully tired. Picture Oz's Dorothy dropping in the field of poppies. My extreme exhaustion was a textbook example of psychological stress expressed in physical terms. Just when I needed to be my most energetic, I could barely move.

Still each time he arrived, I pushed hard and switched into Jonah mode, as though he had never been away. He'd have good and bad days, but we were always on edge, anticipating a possible "bad" period. Those episodes were marked by an uncomfortable restlessness, when he'd pace endlessly avoiding touch or gentle guidance, refusing to sit, lie down or eat. Sleep was out of the question. He'd become agitated and, short of sitting in the car, he did nothing but walk and throw the things we offered. Flying plates of food provided comic relief for his brother and sister, but it was hard to watch how uncomfortable Jonah was in his own skin. There was no anticipating or stopping these episodes once they began— they took on a life of their own. It was as though some enzyme or hormone had been released into his system and had to work its way out. Medication, at best, slowed him down but made him dizzy and more prone to falling, not a great side effect for someone as clumsy as Jonah. I used the term "seizure like" to describe these episodes to the neurologist not realizing that an official introduction to epilepsy would soon follow.

It was an unusually hot summer day and Jonah seemed off, perhaps ill. He was warm to the touch so I bathed him in lukewarm water and put him on the couch with a favorite movie. Instead of watching, his eyes froze upward. He began jerking, rhythmically, going in and out of consciousness. Unable to reach the phone, I held him close, and cried. Thankfully a babysitter for the other children arrived and I was able to bring him to the hospital. There, the physician on call made it official—Jonah had developed epilepsy.

I was surprised seizures could begin so late in the game but among individuals with autism this was common. He was almost twelve and would need to take medication daily, probably for the rest of his life. His seizures were considered "classic" and the neurologist prescribed Dilantin. We had no way of knowing that Jonah was severely allergic to almost all the first line drugs used to treat epilepsy. Angry skin rashes developed all over his body and required steroid shots which triggered wild behavior. He moved frantically for days making the side effects of treatment worse than the ailment. Settling him down over the next two weeks was hellish.

Mix and match, trial and error— that was the dark hole we were asked to look down in trying to figure out what medication or combination of drugs would work. Even if he was controlled, doctors told us, breakthrough seizures were likely. How often? How severe? No one could say. All we knew for sure was that now, with seizures, there were additional safety concerns. He'd need constant monitoring and one- to-one supervision around the clock.

Almost one year later, before his 13th birthday, we prepared for his return home for summer break. The usual hoopla preceded his arrival but the school nurse had called the week before to report that Jonah, even with increased supervision, had fallen. We knew from experience that he was a slip and fall kind of guy, seeing only what he wanted, never the things that were in his way. We'd had many rides to the emergency room and knew any scans or x-rays would require general anesthesia, heavy artillery for a routine test. Hoping to avoid a hospital ordeal, the nurse agreed to follow Jonah closely for the next hours and days. She phoned often assuring me that Jonah was fine, "up to his old tricks." I believed her and besides, he'd be home in a few days. I would be able to judge for myself.

When he returned home, he looked fine and seemed in good spirits until I noticed clear watery fluid pooling in the crevice above his upper lip. This was eerily different than mucous. I was alarmed thinking that it might be related to his fall.

Because professionals stay away from treating their own it was always me, not Mike, who figured out that Jonah's sour breath equaled strep throat; that quietude and over compliance meant it was time to start the Tylenol and that head scratching could mean a headache or an allergic skin rash. I raised the possibility of a connection between the mysterious drip from his nose and his recent fall and Mike agreed, Jonah should be checked out.

It didn't take long to confirm, and after tests and more tests we were told he had a cerebral spinal fluid (CSF) leak, a result of a hairline fracture of the skull. Fluid that surrounded his brain was slowly seeping through the break and out of his nose. I felt horrible for having sent him to Higashi where this happened, conveniently forgetting how many close calls we'd had at home. But more urgent issues about what to do were pressing; decisions needed to be made.

We were told that on occasion such fractures healed spontaneously, but if left unsealed predisposed Jonah to an increased risk of meningitis. Surgery was recommended, but once again, there would be no guarantees.

We wanted to be told what to do, but ultimately the decision was ours. Jonah had spent a fair amount of time in hospital emergency rooms getting fingers stitched, sedated for episodes and treated for prolonged seizures. But the thought of him being hospitalized with no definitive promise of recovery was hard to fathom. Surgery meant Jonah would remain in the ICU under general anesthesia for an impossible-to-determine length of time. That alone presented risks that were hard to assess.

We opted for the surgery. Mike and I spent the next month in Detroit's Children Hospital learning the hospital system from the patient's perspective. Many specialists cared for Jonah, each with differing and sometimes conflicting opinions. But there was no one person managing, overseeing various elements of his care. I likened it to an orchestra with great musicians but no conductor, lots of noise without music. Once again there were questions without answers accompanied by an endless stream of forms that needed to be signed. It was the first time in Michael's career that he got to see the kind of frustrations and bureaucracies patients had to deal with.

After nearly a month, I was still spending my days in the ICU with Jonah. September 27th was his 13th birthday, the day that, under different circumstances would have been his Bar Mitzvah. No one remembered. I prayed by his bedside overwhelmed by feelings. I remembered the day of his naming and how I imagined him standing beside his father reading from the Torah. I looked at him hooked up to tubes and monitors and thought about all that had happened in his short life, how changed we were and how many good deeds he enabled us to do by being a part of our family.

In the adjacent room I heard a woman crying, another mother, I learned, whose son had died earlier that day. Being so preoccupied with Jonah for so long had narrowed my scope, made me unable to see adversity's broad strokes and the heavy load others, like her, were forced to shoulder.

We were two mothers, in separate rooms, with separate lives. But September 27th would forever be marked on our calendars, me for a birth, and she for a death. Jonah would not have a Bar Mitzvah. There would be no Torah reading, speech or merrymaking. Yet hearing this woman made me realize that, when all was said and done, indeed I had something to celebrate.

"Cows in Canada"

Jonah was discharged from the hospital without definite answers about the surgery's outcome. Once all the internal swelling went down we would know more. That could take months. In the meantime the doctors said "goodbye" and expected us to pick up our lives where we left off.

Jonah, however, had become a different child; thin and weak with eyes that seemed to register nothing. Basic functions we had come to take for granted, chewing food, drinking from a cup and walking unattended, disappeared. The month-long hospitalization had erased Jonah's most basic skills much like the sliding button on his doodling toy made his scribbles vanish. For the first time those who had referred to Jonah as "sick" were correct.

We'd had our share of despairing moments before but seeing what Jonah could no longer do made us realize how much we'd taken for granted. His favorite videos inspired none of the usual excitement. The fork we handed him fell between his fingers to the floor. We were devastated. In the past Mike and I took turns with tears, one remaining supportive while the other fell apart. This time we cried together.

We called the surgeon hoping to hear words of encouragement but instead received ambiguity and evasions. When David and Ruth asked if Jonah would be okay, we responded with tempered optimism. This was familiar territory—the land of questions without answers. Though we knew there were no guarantees, we wanted to believe that a good outcome was more probable than possible. Only Jonah's pediatrician seemed to understand this and offered support. She explained that especially for children like Jonah, regression after a long hospitalization was common. Typically, she told us, they regained function over time. We clung to her words.

Emotional stress compounded with the physical demands of caring for Jonah had taken its toll. Life was anything but usual, yet we tried to sustain some level of normalcy for our other children. We whispered and tiptoed around Jonah, watching videos, pushing him in a wheelchair and feeding him meals while trying to reacquaint him with old skills. His progress was painfully slow—he stood up; took a few steps; urinated in the toilet. But it was when he held his fork independently for the first time that we knew he was getting back on track.

Nothing could have made us happier. Slowly the haze of illness lifted and Jonah reemerged, a sluggish version of his old self. We felt as though we had been given a second chance.

Careful not to push, we allowed him to move forward at his own pace. But after turning a corner, it seemed he wanted to make up for lost time. Suddenly he was leaping ahead, full throttle. We were caught off guard, totally drained from all that we had been through. Jonah needed us to be one step ahead and we could barely keep up. This went on for weeks. We didn't want to send him back to Higashi but there wasn't much choice; we were completely burnt out. There was no way we could continue caring for him at home.

Ours was an "impossible situation," whatever choice we made would not be what we wanted. Keep him home and we would buckle under the stress of caring for him. Send him back to school and I would be entrusting him to the people who allowed this mishap to occur.

For so long we'd put Jonah's interests before our own; devoted ourselves to making the world fit his needs. But things had changed. Besides other children, we had our marriage and ourselves to consider. Telling people that the school provided superior education and round-the-clock-care sounded like an empty public relations pitch. All you had to do was look at us to know that Jonah had to go back to Higashi and why.

Staff at Higashi were glad to seem him, relieved that they weren't being sued for Jonah's accident. We were sad yet anxious to get back to a routine. We said goodbye to Jonah, and as I exited the building, I breathed deeply, something, once again, I hadn't done in months.

The next morning after arriving home I went for a walk alone. It felt like I had missed an entire season of living. I'd walked the route with Jonah in his wheelchair countless times, but this was the first time in months that I was able to actually see what was around me.

I arrived home and in tribute to Jonah, tackled the physical chaos with Mary-Poppins like, finger-snapping abandon. Able to transform the environment in such a dramatic way made me feel empowered and reassured. I went through the mail, arranged long overdue appointments and reconnected with people I had no time for before. Once I was back to some routine, I saw the word "relief" spelled out in neon pink, flashing, capital letters in my mind. There was nothing subtle about the change.

Adjusting emotionally was harder. I couldn't use the word "happy" to describe how we felt about our decision, yet knew there were no better alternatives. I wanted to do what was right for all of us but there was no getting away from the feeling that ultimately Jonah paid the biggest price.

I found it difficult to call the school, afraid of hearing bad news or a judging voice on the other end. The guilt about sending him back to the place where the accident occurred plagued me. When Michael called, I'd stand by the phone anxious to hear what was going on, relying on him to temper any bad news he might hear. The next time I would see Jonah was when he returned home for vacation.

The school's year-end celebration, a show that featured group and individual performances by Higashi students, marked the beginning of the spring break. Those who could, sang, danced, did acrobatics, played musical instruments while those who were less able, like Jonah, jumped on a pogo stick or rode a bike across the stage. Instead of the proverbial fifteen minutes, each student got a few seconds of fame.

Members of the press and local community were invited and applauded along with families and staff. For the grand finale all classes gathered on stage for one last song. My tall handsome son was lined up in back, looking everywhere but where he was supposed to, the only one with an aide holding on to him. Even among a hundred plus children with autism, Jonah's need for supervision was evident.

We went straight to the airport after the show and I was happy to see Jonah looking and behaving much like he did before his accident. We'd stocked the refrigerator with favorite treats, bought magazines and tried to anticipate what he might enjoy. After a remarkably smooth first week, however, things fell apart. He was bigger, we were older. Agitated, sleepless and uncomfortable, Jonah's new difficult behavior was throwing himself to the ground. We'd already experienced what it was like for him to have a major head injury. I was unnerved.

There was no way to figure out what was bothering him. I thought of all the uncomfortable sensations he might be feeling but was unable to express. What if he had a mouth full of canker sores when he drank the orange juice I'd given him that morning. Maybe he felt nauseated or had a migraine headache that had been aggravated by the outdoor sunshine. There were never answers, just conjecture. I gave him Tylenol to cover all pain bases, but the behavior persisted. I was frustrated but Jonah was the one who suffered autism's ultimate cruelty by being unable to communicate.

After two nights of struggling to keep him from hurting himself, we brought him to the hospital emergency room. He was frightened and uncontrollable, flailing and diving to the floor. He was all noise and motion so that security, not surprisingly, was called. I protested as the brutish guards, twice his size strong-armed him. He became more agitated and resistive when they put him in restraints but no one listened as I begged them to back off. Jonah looked to me for help but there was nothing I could do. I felt like the wicked stepmother in a nightmarish fairytale. Even with Michael standing beside me, I felt small and alone.

It was a miserable night and when we left hours later, Jonah was draped over the side of the wheelchair, heavily sedated. I walked out of the hospital with a prescription in my purse but no advice on how to manage such frightening episodes. Even medicated, Jonah tried throwing himself, head first to the ground. The only difference was that he moved in slow motion.

We'd had our fill of consultations with top experts, but we were desperate. I called a friend for the number of a doctor she had been urging me to see. His name had come up many times before but his expertise was medication, one of my least favorite things to impose on Jonah. The doctor had a child with autism and supposedly had a gift for understanding the subtleties of hard-to-treat situations such as this.

He squeezed us in for an emergency appointment taking copious notes while Jonah paced back and forth, unable to sit even for a moment. When Jonah grabbed and threw the doctor's eyeglasses, he didn't flinch. I was glad the man got to see a true picture of what we were dealing with.

I questioned whether Jonah's diminished speech might be contributing to the problem. After years of being bombarded with language, perhaps he was on overload, unable to access the few words he knew how to use. Maybe this behavior was his way of expressing his frustration with lost speech.

The doctor seemed amused by my suggestion and said language acquisition was cumulative in all people including those with autism. Loss of speech, according to him, was atypical though I had many friends who had seen

.he same thing in their children with autism. He cited his own child as an example, who spoke in full sentences and had improved so much that he considered his child to have "part-time autism." With that comment I was reminded why I stopped consulting experts.

Still I wanted the magic pill we had come for. Surely there was something in one of the thick volumes on the doctor's sagging shelves that could rescue Jonah from this periodic misery. He scribbled something on his pad and handed me a prescription for the same sedative Jonah had been given at the hospital. I'd later learn that only a handful of medicines treated such problems. The art was finding the right dose and combination. There were no magic pills.

We waited things out, watching as Jonah battled his demons. It was hard for us, but harder still for him. It was heartbreaking and seeing Jonah's suffering made it impossible not to ask questions about his quality of life.

How different was Jonah's life from the end stage Alzheimer's patients I sometimes thought might be better off dead? What did this innocent boy hope to achieve or have to look forward to? As his mother, these were questions I had no right to ask, yet seeing his misery made it impossible not to. "All thoughts are allowable," I told my children, "as long as they are not acted upon." Yet I hated what I was thinking. Jonah was such a simple human being and managed to generate some of life's most complex ethical and philosophical questions.

I knew there were no "good" answers, yet a car ride through Canada would unexpectedly help me understand the purpose of Jonah's life. The road we traveled ran through farm country and every few miles we'd see cows grazing. Some were clustered, others stood alone. Even the loud noise of passing transport trucks did not cause them to look up from their grazing. They were on autopilot; nature had programmed them in a way that reduced their lives to compliance and a simple series of steps. They were herded, set out to pasture, milked and basically lived each day, content with what the average human being would consider a joyless existence. They produced dairy products, meat and leather goods, and yet they lived contentedly oblivious to their contribution.

How different was Jonah's life? Every hour in his day was guided by others and his pleasures, simple and few, were hard to gauge and comprehend. That he did not understand the impact of his presence, did not devalue his role. Though they seemed unremarkable at first, these cows in Canada became an unforgettable symbol of Jonah's part in the world. And though I thought my connection between cows and autism was serendipitous, I would later learn that Temple Grandin, a well-known speaker and writer with autism, has become a leading designer of humane equipment for farm animals because of her ability to "think like a cow."

The newness of Jonah's episode left us feeling off kilter, but after a few days the hysteria finally remitted. But unlike its start, which was sudden, the near hysteria faded off, gradually. With the agitation gone, he became quiet and subdued and allowed me to touch him for the first time in days. I held him close, sad yet relieved, wanting so much to be able to shield him from future pain. It was a mother's wish I knew would never come true.

Jonah Now

It was easy to idealize life with Jonah when he was away at school— to forget the commotion, frayed nerves and sleepless nights. I missed him as weeks between visits passed, feeling his absence whenever I left his place at the table unset or wrote four instead of five in the space marked "number of guests" on response cards. I longed for small things— his warmth beside me, his soft carpet of hair to tussle, the scent that was his alone.

I put photographs of him all over the house, reminders of moments; when I made him smile by playing favorite Disney video segments or got him to look at the camera by holding a box of donuts over my head. The real Jonah, however, was captured in the four by six photos of him turning away, his black olive-shaped eyes gazing at something nobody else could see. These images, candid and poignant, evoked a sense of sadness and loss that would never disappear.

Family gatherings intensified the feelings. Each year we flew to Florida for the Passover holiday, conscious that 20 percent of my family was back in Boston. During the Seder, the celebratory meal, we'd talk about the symbolic significance of the exodus from Egypt. What aspects of our lives from the previous year would we leave behind and where were we hoping to go. But instead of contributing to the conversation I'd fixate on the Haggadic passages about one of the four sons—the one "who did not know how to ask." Naturally the reference made me think of Jonah and how he was eating bread in his dormitory rather than matzo with us. There wasn't a day that I didn't feel the weight of my decision. This was the price I'd chosen to pay.

Friends had to adapt to the changes in our lives as well. Some weren't sure how to handle Jonah's absence. Should they avoid talking about him? Was this a case of out of sight out of mind? People thought nothing of asking the cost of Jonah's tuition or telling us that "it was about time we got a life." Fortunately we knew to take cloddish opinions and judgments lightly, observing that the people we cared least about seemed to have the most to say. We finally could relate to how mourners felt when they were told lost loved ones were "better off."

Those who spoke from the heart got it right. They'd ask how Jonah was doing, or acknowledge how hard it must be for us to have him so far away. Their support and honest expression of feeling meant so much. They also understood that Jonah's deficits and compromised life would always be a source of sadness for us. They didn't talk about time "healing" our "wounds" or finally finding "closure." Jonah's autism, they recognized, was not something we could store in a box and place in some unused closet.

We visited Jonah at school between breaks as often as we could, but getting away became increasingly difficult. Besides finding time off from work and care for our younger children, there were the usual complications of flying—weather, delays, cancellations. Even when our travels went smoothly, the hassles far outweighed the little bit of time we actually got to spend with Jonah.

We'd return home tired and frustrated, resuming the countdown till his next visit home. My calendar, normally filled with scribbled notes and appointments, was blank from a week before his arrival until a week after his departure. When Jonah was headed home everything else in my life was placed on hold.

Food canisters, cookie jars and fruit bowls were cleared from the kitchen. Breakables were stored in an out of the way closet. Jonah's videos, dust collectors while he was away, were organized and made ready for use. The children were reminded to put away all school projects and game pieces. Things we hadn't thought about in months became safety considerations. Our preparations suggested that we were expecting more than a visit from a family member on school break.

Remarkably, he would walk through the door and it would feel as though he never left. We'd take our places and know intuitively who needed to watch Jonah while another person set the table or answered the phone. After a few reasonably calm days he would go into overdrive. My joke that his energy could electrify a small city still applied. With each visit Jonah grew bigger and stronger while we became older and slower. Getting the help we needed continued to be a logistical nightmare.

Working with Jonah was not a job one could easily jump into. Any new person needed time to gain his trust, know him well enough to understand his unspoken language. We finally met Tony, a Higashi staffer who didn't mind spending his vacation time off with our family.

Tony was a big boisterous in-your-face fellow who, unlike any caregiver before, gave Jonah's a boy's life. Jonah got to sit behind the steering wheel in Maserati and Jaguar showrooms, attended big league sports events and rode the most daring amusement park rides. Never shy to share his thoughts, Tony challenged strangers who looked disapprovingly at Jonah asking, "Didn't your parents teach you that it is not nice to stare?" He was a good fit with our family and was fun but exhausting to be around. After he and Jonah went back to Higashi, it took a week to reclaim the calm we'd grown accustomed to and savored.

Jonah's progress at Higashi was modest, at best, and after five years of believing we might still see improvement, I felt I wanted him back in Michigan. I also knew he could no longer live with us. He was 16 at the time, two years short of the 18 required to qualify for the funding necessary for housing and care. That gave me two years to pull together three major pieces— schooling, dwelling and, most importantly, care giving. I had my work cut out for me.

Initially I thought we were lucky to live in a state and district that, besides providing education until age 26, offered a choice of programs. But what Jonah needed still didn't exist. The center programs were joyless arrangements, with indifferent staff and a warehouse atmosphere. We were unimpressed seeing students cramped in small or windowless rooms, a certain disaster for someone like Jonah who, more than anything needed space to move around.

We were told Jonah could be included in a regular education high school. I visited the school, surpriscd to see a former classmate of Jonah's in the program. A lecture on monsoons in China was being given, while the young woman stared off in another direction. It was difficult not to wonder how this young woman related to this subject. What would be the point of putting Jonah into a program such as this? What would I be proving? Mike and I didn't care about appearances; all we were concerned with was serving Jonah's best interests.

Excluding inclusion from school options reminded us of not having Jonah participate in the region's Special Olympics. Besides not understanding the meaning of competition or winning, Jonah hates crowds, noise and being handled. He has always been a great swimmer but getting trophies and being fussed over mean nothing to him. As much as I would have loved to see Jonah standing in a winner's circle, I refused to make an activity he enjoyed agenda-driven.

For him, to be included would be similar. It didn't matter if something sounded great or made sense for others—the question we always asked ourselves was whether Jonah would benefit. It appeared that, at least school-wise, we were on the road to nowhere.

Anxious to move forward, we turned our attention to finding a house. We wanted Jonah to live in a place as comfortable as our home but, because of his seizures, without steps. The only way I could ensure this was for me to purchase a home he could then rent from me. I would become a landlord, adding one more hat to the many I'd already worn for Jonah's benefit.

At first I didn't think roommates would be a good idea but logistically and financially sharing a home made more sense. Even though Jonah didn't speak, he needed the stimulation of being spoken to. Also, additional people living in the home meant more staff would be needed. This would lessen the risk of burn out. Roommates would also allow expenses to be shared.

I didn't want Jonah to live too close to us, fearful that I would feel guilty about not spending every free moment I had with him. I also didn't want to feel that I had to go over every time I made a pot of soup or baked something. As fate would have it, the place we found was about one mile away.

I was tentative at first, but homes with our specifications were in short supply. The close proximity turned out to be a blessing in disguise. Being less than five minutes away now allows us to be spontaneous, and I like dropping off the soup and cookies I had been afraid of obligating me. It is a luxury being able to see him or give him a goodnight kiss on a whim and know that if he is not in the mood for us, we can leave without feeling like we've sacrificed a lot of time traveling.

Once we had solid ideas about the right house, we turned our attention to providers, those people in charge of managing Jonah's daily routine. A home, we knew, was only as good as its caregivers. Ultimately those who worked with Jonah would make or break the success of his transition back to Michigan. Finding the right people would be key.

Kindness and patience topped our list of requirements. Experience had taught us to look beyond the superficial—piercings and tattoos may have not been our style, but they did not disguise a warm smile and gentle manner. Anyone willing to take time to know Jonah, understand his wants and be a little bit of mother, father, sister, brother and friend rolled into one was ideal.

We had to think along the same lines as the administrators who recruited and managed the caregivers. Philosophically there were providers who were relaxed in their management style allowing clients, like Jonah, to call the shots. Jonah however did not make clear choices and needed structure and consistency above all else. Besides, a "hang loose" style could never work for two Type A personalities like Michael and me, who were happiest when I's were dotted and T's crossed. We hoped for consistent, reliable people who would follow up on problems and be open to our input. Given the constant budget slashing and the limits of Jonah's funding they needed to be fiscally responsible and judicious about assigning the right people to his care.

The way to get a sense of the providers was to visit the homes they ran. We knew single visits never told the whole story, but they provided snapshots, sometimes the kind that made us never want to go back. Though many clients could not speak, how they were dressed, body language, the upkeep of the home spoke volumes. I observed staff attitudes and interactions and stayed to see what was served for meals. Some places seemed overcrowded and disorganized; others well kept but lacking in the warmth I wanted Jonah to have.

We walked into the home we liked best as a staff person was putting the finishing touches on a client's manicure.

The other women who lived there smiled as they modeled their polished nails for me. Framed photos of the women on outings and with family members decorated the walls. They ate dinner with staff and talked with an ease and familiarity that created a sense of family. The company that oversaw that home would eventually take charge of Jonah's care.

Though I had gotten the ball rolling for Jonah's return home, there was still the financial front to address. I became a businesswoman, a player who targeted the right people to get things done. I learned to advocate without becoming adversarial, but wasn't shy about asking for legal help when necessary. I navigated a tangle of bureaucracies that redefined the words "frustrating" and "illogical."

For Jonah to qualify for funding, for example, I was told to portray him as an impossible to care for nightmare. To get an agency to agree to take him on, however, I was told to whitewash things. They could refuse him if they saw him as being too challenging. I was told to contradict myself, say opposite things to different people. But just as I was unwilling to make excuses for Jonah in the past, I would not mislead and exaggerate. Truth was my ally and how I said things counted as much as what was said. I painted Jonah as he was, a sweet, lovable young man who was dealt a challenging hand for which he needed help. That's why these people I appealed to were so important. It took two solid years to lay the groundwork for Jonah's future with new chapters in an ongoing story ready to begin.

Every Child
is Born to Matter

W hen *Rain Man* was released in 1988, I avoided the
film, afraid to see how Hollywood would treat a
subject so close to my heart. Besides, at that time, going
to the movies was a chance for me to escape, not to watch
my personal life on a public screen. But I was wrong. That
one of its main characters had autism was almost beside
the point—what grabbed me was the story about a shared
journey, familial love and personal transformation.

In the movie, Charlie is a self-absorbed car salesman
who, like his autistic older brother Raymond (*Rain Man)*
has difficulty developing relationships. The smooth talker
is unaccustomed to not getting what he wants and learns,
especially in dealing with his autistic brother, none of the
usual rules apply. By the film's end, Raymond, without

intending to, helps Charlie become a better person. Jonah's impact on our family has been similar.

When I whine or feel cheated, for example, Jonah prompts me to look again. Every day he is tested and frustrated with ample reason to be angry and aggressive. Yet he is a placid, gentle soul who will take the hand of anyone who reaches out to him. Seeing what he deals with each day trivializes our complaints and reminds us to keep life's headaches in their proper perspective.

Because of Jonah the most modest achievements appear grand in scale. When he was away at school, I'd want to "talk" to him. I was content to hear him breathing, making noise in the background, even throwing the receiver to the ground. We'd tried teaching him to say, " I love you," by starting him off with the word "I," and having him fill in the subsequent two words. In person the exchange sometimes worked, but never on the phone. Still each time I called, I'd venture an "I," never counting on a response until one day he surprised me with an unexpected "lob-you." I was thrilled. That single run on word uttered in his trademark monotone was his gift to me—great news I shared with closest friends and family. Few people could relate to my happiness.

While Jonah's ability to go after things he wants without contemplating consequences can be, especially in dangerous situations, vexing, it has also been inspiring. On a recent visit to Jonah's home, for example, I brought a few boxes of his favorite cereal. He was dozing on the couch, so I left the bag and went to talk with staff in the kitchen. Soon after I heard Jonah vocalizing from his bathroom in the back of the house. His hand was deep in the bag of cereal he'd opened, the emptied box at his feet. Crumbs clung to his wet cheeks. I laughed, liking that he'd gone after what he wanted and "hid" in a place he knew his privacy would be respected. "Seized moments" such as these, remind us —people governed by rules and regulations – to occasionally, throw caution to the wind.

Because of Jonah we learned to consider what's right for our family without worrying about appearances or opinions of others. For years I wasn't comfortable taking family vacations without him. As if having a disabled child was not guilt-inducing enough, the thought of leaving him behind while we enjoyed time away seemed unconscionable. Jonah, however, likes what he knows, and removing him from his familiar environment and routines made him miserable. It took several fiasco trips for me to see that he had no interest in the things I wanted to share. Not being in family pictures, I finally realized, didn't mean he wasn't a part of our family portrait.

Even though he spent so much time away, Jonah's impact on his siblings, David and Ruth, was profound. They remember the years Jonah lived at home; the stream of people and accompanying hoopla; the laughter Jonah precipitated by throwing things into a crowd or grabbing food from unsuspecting strangers. A bad case of gas gave them something to laugh about all day. They admired his disregard for manners and behavioral protocol and his ability to get away with all kinds of mischief.

They became more compassionate and patient because of Jonah. Even as small children, David and Ruth generously stepped aside to give him center stage with maturity far beyond their years. They had compassion for others who struggled and when they started school, teachers often paired them with the students who needed extra help.

They readily introduced their older brother when friends visited, glad for a chance to explain autism. They respected Jonah's dignity and objected whenever they heard someone using the word "retard" thoughtlessly. They applauded Jonah's achievements, focused on his strengths yet understood, from very early on, the fruitlessness of anger directed at him.

They also remember the anxiety and sense of helplessness that permeated the household. They worried about his seizures which were frighteningly dramatic and unpredictable. Before returning home for vacations, they didn't like hearing that "Jonah has to come first" during his time home. Especially in the early years, they were afraid that changes to accommodate him might become permanent.

Jonah's absence may have protected them from feeling chronically displaced, but there was a tradeoff. No matter how many times we explained why and how it was difficult for us to send Jonah away to school, they worried that they might face a similar fate. They'd act out, push hard, test boundaries—our reassurance doing little to quiet what to them were logical worries. The precedent set with Jonah took its toll even in indirect ways.

Despite the compromises and concessions each of us made, it was made clear that Jonah was no one's responsibility but ours. I sheltered David and Ruth from feeling burdened, paying for the extra hands I needed so that their help could be offered rather than demanded. By arranging for Jonah's future we felt we were preparing for theirs. They were told repeatedly that Jonah's necessities were and would continue to be provided for and that they would not be limited geographically because of their brother. Despite all of this, I am touched by how often they talk about including Jonah in their futures. "Every family needs a bachelor uncle," they agree. They are growing into two truly spectacular people.

Though he is still young, David talks about a career in neurology and spends time with disabled adults besides Jonah. Ruth's very first cry after birth was a declaration that she would be heard. She is a keen observer, tireless fighter and feels driven to right the worlds' wrongs. She and David are united, especially in Jonah matters, yet as typical teens, argue about almost everything else. Wearing as the petty quarreling can become, having Jonah makes me appreciate the "normality" of their behavior. There is some truth to my tease that their bickering makes Jonah sometimes feel "like my easy child." He, after all, is fine as long as there is food, comfort and caring whereas with David and Ruth, I have to tread lightly, with everything becoming a matter of discussion or negotiation.

They worry knowing that there is no prenatal screening for autism and that they have an increased risk for having a child with the disability. I wish I could paint "happily ever after" endings for them, but they know there are no guarantees. "We handled it and if G-d forbid you have to, you will too," I tell them. Their futures, I remind them, are blank canvasses —they are free to imagine anything. "Choose the positive," I encourage, "and pray for good outcomes. The rest is out of your hands."

Fortunately in recent years autism has become the darling of disabilities, gracing covers of national news magazines and capturing headlines on network news and morning shows. Books have been written about people with autism people who recover (*Son-Rise*, by Barry Neil Kaufman), have unique communication skills (*Facilitated Communication Training*, by Rosemary Crossley), or make remarkable gains despite the difficult odds (*Let me Hear Your Voice: A Family's Triumph Over Autism*, by Catherine Maurice). Higher functioning individuals with autism are also the focus of the film *Rain Man* and the book *The Curious Incident of the Dog in the Night*. Asperger's syndrome, considered a "less severe form of autism," also receives an enormous amount of attention.

While any publicity is supposedly "good publicity," these portraits tend to overlook the thousands of individuals who, like Jonah, are more severely affected by autism. Unfortunately, many never develop spontaneous speech, master self-help skills or achieve independence. Jonah's neurologist described autism as a "wastebasket term," because of the dramatic discrepancies between individuals with the same diagnosis. A person with a Ph.D. in math and a nonverbal adult in diapers can both have autism. With a skyrocketing statistic of one in 150 being diagnosed with the disability (as opposed to 15 in 10,000 when Jonah was first born) one wonders what has changed.

Personally, I don't doubt the possibility that environmental, biological, toxic factors may contribute to the escalation in numbers of people being diagnosed with autism. But I also believe that the criteria for diagnosis has been broadened, and that the label is given more casually than it was in the past. We all have our fixations, repetitive behaviors. Some of us thrive on routine and get upset when things are off schedule or prefer books and objects to the company of people. Others are poor at picking up social cues, don't respect personal space and talk long after the listener wishes the conversation had ended. Genius math and science professors without lives outside their labs or the wherewithal to match shoes before leaving the house would have been called "eccentric" in previous generations. Now they might be counted among those who contribute to the autism statistics.

The skyrocketing numbers are alarming, but what is even more disturbing is how much remains unknown about autism's causes and treatment. Leo Kanner first described the disability in 1943, and contrary to what some reports suggest, autism does not respond consistently to any known remedies. Of course there are people who swear by the positive effects of restrictive diets, chelation, ABA training, auditory integration therapy, facilitated communication – the list goes on. And though none of these things worked for Jonah, I never question the veracity of claims. I respect the individuality of this disability and the different ways people approach it, especially since nothing that is tried is easy. Perhaps there will be better answers in the near future. The recently passed Combating Autism Act of 2006 authorized nearly $1 billion in spending to fight autism over the next five years. The funds will be used to increase public awareness and provide enhanced federal support for research and treatment. For now, however, parents are left without solid answers.

So many variables go into shaping a life and Jonah's story is his alone. He had two parents who worked together and a budget that allowed us to pay for help we needed; yet others with fewer resources and less support had more success with the same interventions we tried. We did what we felt was right for Jonah, readily admitting that no decision or outcome was perfect. Would he have been worse off had we not tried the things we did? We'll never know.

Still, I consider Jonah luckier than most being born in a generation of children raised by parents who have established strong bonds and plan to remain involved for their lifetimes. This development will hopefully change the long-term quality of care for the tens of thousands like Jonah who have no place to spend their time once the school years end. Funding is the ever-present albatross of the special needs world and, as a result, marginal programs are justified because of the large number of people they serve.

At one time we wanted to start a farm cooperative, perhaps in partnership with a university. Staff could be drawn from students interested in special education, psychology, social work, physical and occupational therapies. Agricultural students could run the farm while business students could manage the accounting end of things. Hands-on training for a variety of majors would be available. The residents could have quiet productive lives, working on the farm, selling their goods. But when I asked an agency head about developing such an arrangement I was told "the days of funny farms are over." This unwillingness to think outside the bureaucratic box is shortsighted but typical. Lack of receptivity to new ideas makes it very difficult to create and implement alternative programming. Consequently, the farm remains a dream that has yet to be realized.

In the meantime Jonah's life is quite full. He shares a home with two twenty-somethings and attends a day program that respects his changing moods and abilities. He keeps a busy schedule that includes swimming, horseback riding and hiking Michigan's scenic trails. We call often and try to see him at least once a week. Though we are familiar with his range of behaviors, he remains a shoot-from-the-hip young man who keeps those around him on their toes. These days his periods of seeming comfortable in his own skin appear to be getting longer, something I thank G-d for every day.

It's hard to look at Jonah and not wonder what he might have become, as a person, husband, father, professional. Even after all that we've been through I sometimes wonder if the past years weren't some heaven-directed scheme meant to humble and teach us. After all, more than anything, Jonah, our accidental teacher, has taught us that sometimes there are no clear answers.

Naturally we still worry about his future, the instability of the ever changing governmental systems that provide for him, the people who, day-to-day, care for him and the impact he will have on the lives of his siblings and their future families. But agonizing about what may be is really a statement about our lack of control. Knowing that things have been set up so that the quality of Jonah's life will be maintained when we are no longer here, is the best we can do for now. Beyond that we choose not to dwell on what might be and try, sometimes not all that successfully, to live in the here and now. The story is far from over.

On a recent visit to New York City my jewelry-loving daughter asked if we could walk around Tiffany's. We stopped to listen as a well-spoken salesman explained the unique attributes of cashew pearls. Asymmetric, dimpled and unusually lustrous, I'd never seen anything like them before. "Nature's anomaly," was how he described these rare jewels. And I was reminded of Jonah.